BOUQUET

OTHER BOOKS BY G. B. STERN

DEBATABLE GROUND

THE ROOM

THE BACK SEAT

SMOKE RINGS

THE MATRIARCH

THUNDERSTORM

THE CHINA SHOP

A DEPUTY WAS KING

THE DARK GENTLEMAN

HOTEL DE FRANCE

ANGLADE, Propriétaire

PLACE DE L'HOTEL-DE-VILLE, **SAUGUES** (HAUTE-LOIRE)

ÉLECTRICITÉ - GARAGE   BUREAU des AUTOBUS
CUISINE SOIGNÉE   DE LANGEAC

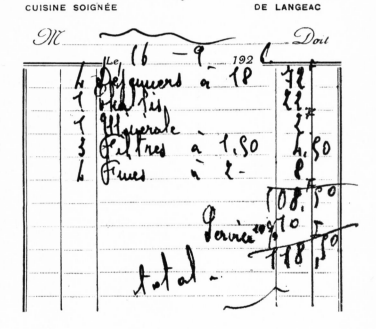

OUR BILL AT THE INN OF LEGEND

G. B. STERN

BOUQUET

NEW YORK

ALFRED · A · KNOPF

1927

TO

ROSEMARY, HUMPHREY

AND

JOHNNY

SEPTEMBER 5TH-OCTOBER 8TH

1926

CONTENTS

CONTENTS

CONTENTS

ILLUSTRATIONS

ILLUSTRATIONS

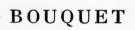

BOUQUET

I
THE FIRST DRINK TOGETHER

I HAVE had so much work to do that I have not had time to get drunk for several weeks, and, signore, my health is suffering from it."

So said my Italian gardener, and these homely yet eloquent words seem to me an apt beginning for a book which is mainly devoted to wine. For though in the pages that follow there is mention of many other things: of food — oh, a lot about food of great succulence! — of swift runs in a long red Fiat, along straight French roads, of hills and rivers and little honey-coloured towns, of heaths and forests and flowers; yet Bacchus is the hero of this book, and a great love of wine its excuse for being written.

It is with diffidence that I, a woman, write in praise of wine. So many crusted connoisseurs believe that the ladies — God bless 'em! — are always happy if you give them Champagne, or a sweetish white wine like Barsac — and finish up with crême de menthe because it's such a pretty colour!

The audacity! Have I not drunk a white Hermitage of 1874? Have I not had Romanée-Conti poured into a great tulip-shaped flagon by a man who had cooked for an emperor? And you would fob me off with Barsac! Even Château Yquem — but we are still a long way from Bordeaux, and the heresies that I shall presently utter against the monarch of Sauternes.

I cannot quite remember when we first had the idea of going on a wine-tour at the time of the vintage. It must have tumbled out very swiftly following our first meeting with Humphrey and Rosemary, because our first talk together was all of wine. They had been motoring through France into Italy, and had stayed at Mâcon, where they drank a certain wonderful Romanée-Conti; and at Tain l'Hermitage, and Pouilly-sur-Loire, at which latter place they "discovered" — everybody "discovers," sooner or later! — a most delicious dry white wine, with a very special bouquet; and of course they boasted shamelessly of these experiences. And Johnny and I, secretly envying them,

boasted back again; I had had a great-great-grand-
mother with a vineyard in Hungary, so that I was
pleased to suppose that a feeling for wine ran in my
blood; and moreover, when I was sixteen, I had drunk
Rüdesheim *at* Rüdesheim — though at the moment I
paid no more heed to this than when I ate Gruyère *at*
Gruyère; rather less, in fact, for cheese, so to speak,
was more familiar ground; and anyhow, at Rüdesheim
I had been listening to my first proposal, which
was wine of a different character, and much more
heady. . . .

"Let's go on a wine-tour!" said Johnny, very
soon after this first interchange of careless arrogance.
Johnny was usually the first to say "Let's," and the
results were often extremely expensive, for we prided
ourselves on being the sort of people who did not allow
"Oh, wouldn't it be lovely?" to slide away like water
for a moment cupped in the palms, to be lost ever afterwards in the sands.

So we met at Avignon, in a thunderstorm, on
the evening of September 5th. Rosemary and I had
travelled from London, and met our husbands, who
had driven up the new Fiat from Italy. The new Fiat's
name was Flotsam, because Johnny and I hoped that

we should one day own a companion Fiat ourselves, and call it Jetsam. The trail of Flotsam's wheels ran over many roads, in the weeks that followed. We slept nearly every night in a different place, and wherever we met people to talk to, we talked to them. We are naturally a gregarious quartet; Rosemary speaks French fluently and beautifully, and I fluently and un-beautifully; and Johnny neither fluently nor beauti-fully, but always with a great deal of courage and en-terprise, and the desire at all costs to have his questions heard and to receive intelligent answers to them; and Humphrey speaks French hardly at all, because he says that he has a wooden leg, and that it is bad for his complaint to be made to talk a language with which God has not originally endowed him. And indeed, though it cannot be contradicted that Humphrey did lose a leg in the War, and that he very wisely and charmingly exploits this infirmity to his advantage in small matters, instead of making us all uncomfortable by cheery assertions that other fellows have just as much to put up with, and that it need not prevent him from doing a major share of any tiresome job that comes along, yet it may be explained here — for I have already wandered so far from my original sentence that there is not much hope of looping back to it — that Humphrey's real name is not Humphrey. He had read a book, a winsome and pathetic book, very popular in the late Victorian period, called *Misunderstood*, by Florence Montgomery, in which little Humphrey was bold and wayward, and sometimes rather naughty, but a splendid little fellow underneath, and always misunderstood by those unthinking people who preferred little Miles, his brother, who was meek and good and helpful; and then little Humphrey fell in the pond, trying to save little Miles, and died very slowly on the sofa; and everybody was terribly sorry that they had misunderstood him, when they saw what a fine little chap he was really, and — and —— Well, now you know why we call him Humphrey! It was he who drove the Fiat, and drove it magnificently, so perhaps he may be exempted from talking voluble French to amiable and complimentary wine-merchants.

During those five weeks in France we encountered not only helpful courtesy and friendliness, but an amount of genial goodwill that amazed me. We never announced ourselves beforehand at a single hotel, and with two exceptions we stayed at those that were marked in the Michelin Guide as two-house — they grade from five-house to one-house — yet we always found instantly that we could command clean bedrooms, good beds, and, in the very few hotels where there was no bathroom, at least running hot and cold water; excellent meals, very little delay, and no grumbling from the staff.

We had many discussions, while in the full enjoyment of comfortable meals in France, as to why the English innkeepers had so degenerated from the old traditions of hospitality and good food and bounteous drink for all comers; and Humphrey dated it back as far as the Wars of the Roses, which, he insisted, so broke up those traditions that they were unable to assemble themselves again before the sour descent of Puritanism, which infused into the very soul of our country the idea that it was wrong to care about eating and drinking, and wrong to care about wine and all material inspirations.

Even to the present day, it is " not done " to be artistically interested and curious about what is set before us, either in the house of a friend or on the table of a hostelry. " Hush, darling! Don't make remarks about what is put before you," is a precept early instilled into us, when we throw the plate of tapioca on the floor, and frankly and formally assert that it is horrid; and yet it strikes me that such behaviour in discriminating adults, in almost every English hotel outside London, might go a long way to reform the present state of slovenly incompetence.

At Avignon, we broke the crust of the wine-tour with a couple of bottles of red Châteauneuf du Pape. The first bottle — 1920 Château Rayas — was excellent, soft and round and full-bodied. . . . There really are no words to describe wine, its aroma and flavour and after-taste, beyond those commonly used in wine-merchants' catalogues. I had hoped to invent an entirely fresh set, each term as vivid as it was original; but I soon learnt humility.

The second bottle, which we anticipated with more excitement than the first, because it was a 1904 vintage, tasted of Camembert cheese — Camembert with a very luscious personality! This was my immediate impression, but, being a coward, I waited for the others to speak. If they had chorused: " Isn't it marvellous? Isn't it divine? " I should have held my peace. Of such stuff are heroes made!

Humphrey sniffed suspiciously, twice, then

rolled some of it round on his tongue. And then looked across at Johnny, who was going through the same performance.

"Rather like cheese, isn't it?"

"Hm! Camembert . . ."

"It *is* like cheese," said Rosemary.

I still do not know what had happened to that bottle, for when we told the wine-waiter that we preferred the 1920 to the 1904, he sighed patiently, as wine-waiters will sigh who know that the present generation have no palate, and no recognition of the mellowness of age in wine; and that unsteadied our self-esteem. He suggested that we should drink it while we ate cheese, and see if it improved under those conditions; and certainly, as we ate Rocquefort, the cheesy taste diminished in the wine, and we ended up by being very well pleased with Châteauneuf du Pape, which is far and away the best wine produced in the neighbourhood of Avignon.

My imagination thus warmed and flushed, I began to ponder upon the tour which lay before us; and, hearing Humphrey and Johnny discussing routes and maps and place-names, without actually listening to the sense of their words, I had a vision of what it was all going to be like — a confusion of preconceived notions, other people's books and pictures and anecdotes, all those fluid shapes and colours gradually fusing themselves into a clear panorama. . . .

There would be roads, of course — straight white French roads, with straight stiff poplars lining them on either side for miles and miles and miles. . . . The road from Arras to Bapaume, of Nevinson's picture — everybody knew what roads in France looked like — white, straight; poplars . . .

And then, clotting these roads, little southern towns; cafés with striped awnings, small tables under the plane-trees, at which sleepy men drank *sirops;* sleepy white oxen drawing a cart through the dust of the sleepy main street; the *mairie* . . . Provençal town . . . Motif, " sleepy."

— So that slid to its place in my mental map.

Bordeaux and Burgundy, and the vintage . . . Here, of course, pictures crashed through decorum and became uncontrollably fantastic. You cannot remain sober, remembering that men still tread out the sweetness of grapes with their bare feet, stamping in the juice. Purple grapes . . . Bacchus . . . And then, as to our more personal share in the riot of images, perhaps the proprietor of some famous château, or a grey-bearded wine-merchant, would unlock the door of his most private cellar, and say to us, with exquisite courtesy: " I have here a bottle which is more than fifty years old. It is the last but one of my store " — for even my uplifted conceit, exalted by Châteauneuf du Pape, would not believe that the last bottle of all would be offered! — " the last but one of my store, so I hope you will honour me by . . . ? " Rosemary and Humphrey and Johnny and I all honoured him, and reverently the cork was drawn. . . .

And after wine, or, rather, simultaneously with wine, *la cuisine*. We would draw up, hungry and tired, before quite a tiny inn, in a wholly unimportant little town on our route; and Madame would come forward and say that she regretted, but she could provide no dinner less humble than, shall we say, *omelette* and *poulet en cocotte;* for this was France's variation from the inevitable English offer of gristly mutton and corn-flour shape, world-without-end, and no alternative — except, possibly, greens and stewed prunes.

And perhaps we might even strike that inn, that famous inn of legend, somewhere in France and at the rainbow's end, where we should be given the most marvellous little dinner ever cooked by a *cordon bleu,* and be charged less than three-and-six per head for it; and should refuse for ever afterwards to divulge its whereabouts to our friends. . . .

But now and here, for the lust of showing myself to myself as so much more splendid and generous than my vision of myself, I will give away the name of that famous inn of legend. For it does indeed exist, and you will read all about it later on, and of what we ate there, and what we drank there, and the price of the bill down to the last sou. Saugues is the name of the village, and it is in the Haute-Loire, at an altitude of 960 metres, and 494 kilometres away from Paris; and the inn is called the Hôtel de France, and it is in the Place de l'Hôtel de Ville.

So you may go there yourselves, if you choose. And if you do, remember that I am perhaps the only person in the whole world who would thus have opened the road to a secret treasure-house. And give thanks to me, and drink a health, that my cellars may always be full, and my palate perceptive.

II
RELICS—AND ROSY WINE

THERE are several wines on the Côte-du-Rhône list which are hardly drunk in England at all. To paraphrase the words of the aristocratic schoolboy: "Hermitage we know, Châteauneuf du Pape we have heard of, but what the devil is Tavel? " Yet Tavel is a very pleasant experience to the palate — a *vin rosé*, the clear innocent colour of a pale ruby. It looks very much lighter in substance and body than it really proves to be, so that we were startled at the effect of several glasses of this rose-red charmer. We drove to Tavel from Avignon; it is a village not far away from Villeneuve-les-Avignon, a little fortified town on the opposite bank of the Rhone.

But this was on our second day; on our first day we had lunch at Hiely's, where we were introduced to *cèpes Bordelais*, preceding the *poulet en cocotte* of my anticipation. But perhaps it is offensive to the Bordelais to describe this unique manner of cooking their little fungi, until we actually were served with them in their ultimate perfection at the Chapeau Rouge in Bordeaux. *Poulet en cocotte,* however, with its enticing sauce, containing mushrooms, truffles, carrots, and artichokes, is a dish eaten as often in all parts of France as boiled mutton in England. Mushrooms and truffles are commonplaces in French cooking, so that for months afterwards, when you return to your own country, you go about, lost and bewildered, missing something, and wondering what it is you miss.

We drank a white Saint Péray, another Rhone wine, with our meal, and noticed for the first time the celebrated " gun-flint " flavour. Now, if I were following blindly in the footsteps of all wine-connoisseurs, I should meekly accept this definition of the subtle backwash and taste and smell which you get from the Côte-du-Rhône wines, and principally from Hermitage; but the first metaphor which sprang to my mind was *not* of gun-flint; for one thing, I am not familiar with gun-flint; it is not a smell nor a taste which occurs in one's normal and everyday existence. It does not figure among the condiments on the table, nor do you have vases or hairbrushes made out of gun-flint. Johnny and Humphrey at once recognized the complete aptness of this man-made metaphor, and my invention failed when I tried to produce a description in opposition.

For it is quite unmistakable and amazing, this Côte-du-Rhône backwash, which occurs about twenty seconds after you have rolled your first sip round the tongue, and allowed it reluctantly to pass down your throat. It is not at all straightforward, but as elusive as the strange charm of a woman whose beauty is neither classic nor chocolate-box; as elusive as the queer emotion at sight or smell of the sea, and of the cliffs running down to the sea, when you have sojourned inland for many months; as elusive as the causeless melancholy, which yet gives you happiness, when you suddenly stand still in the woods, and say: " This is autumn! I can feel it in the air." But perhaps it is shorter than all this just to ejaculate " gun-flint," and be done with it, when you taste a true Côte-du-Rhône wine!

I particularly remember this meal at Hiely's, with its oranges and lemons growing all over the wall-paper, because of the invention of the word " shottled," a word which first and last must have saved us a great deal of time and energy during the next five weeks, for we so often had occasion to say " château-bottled " — " Is this wine château-bottled? " " It is château-bottled." " Is this wine shottled? " . . . It is of the utmost importance whether a wine be shottled or not.

Also, discussing our Bacchanalian future, over the *poulet en cocotte*, I reminded the three others of what Warner Allen, the author of *Wines of France*, had told me about the prospects in Cognac. " You won't be able to drink it, of course, as they'll probably offer you about twenty different vintages to taste. You just roll it round your tongue, and spit it out again."

" Not all of it? " protested my companions. " Not the super-Cognacs? Not the 1865, for instance? "

We came to the conclusion that Johnny and Rosemary and I, being passengers, could swallow Cognac to the limits of our decent capacities, but that Humphrey, of course, who drove the car, Humphrey should be hung round and festooned with cuspidors for the whole of the tour, and particularly at Cognac. " Cuspidor " is a beautiful word, with a swaggering suggestion of bull-fights about it: " Enter the picadors and the matadors, and then the cuspidors. . . ."

Avignon is a pleasant town in which to saunter through an idle day. It has a street in it called the rue des Ortolans, which has old doorways with strange, twisted iron knockers, one of them in the shape of a fish biting its own tail. For diversion you can play ducks and drakes with stones springing along the surface of the Rhone, just below the famous bridge on which the courtly ghosts of ladies and gentlemen with powdered hair danced, as in the old nursery rhyme. I heard a tinker singing a Provençal folk-song outside the Palais des Papes; and I succeeded in not entering the Palais des Papes, which shows great strength of mind, and a sad lack of the proper historical spirit. But it was such a colossal building, seen from outside, dazzling white against the deep-blue sky; and it seemed to me that once you fell into the power of a guide, you would walk for miles and miles and miles before he allowed you to escape into the open again. It was better to announce a point of view of passive receptivity, to sit at a little table at one of the cafés lining the wide boulevard, and to think complacently of an immediate future when all one's exercise, in a manner of speaking, was going to be done by car!

In the narrow streets of Avignon I saw the words "*Vive le roi!*" scribbled on the walls over and over again, words that held a thrill of mystery in a republican country; for what king could they mean? King René, perhaps; that Provençal cliché in monarchs, favourite of the mediæval troubadours, whose theory seemed to be, not unlike that of modern theatrical managers: "It's no good giving the public anything original. King René, now, he's a certain draw! Or Queen Jeanne!"

Driving to Tavel, Humphrey and I discussed troubadouring as a profession; on the whole, not a bad one. It was a convention to keep quiet and listen while the troubadours sang interminably, verse after verse — "While I," Humphrey complained, in parenthesis, "can barely command attention for longer than three-quarters of an hour at a stretch!" In fact, they were such privileged persons that I believe they were not beheaded even if they turned peevish, and said: "I will *not* be interrupted!" and: "Let me finish what I have begun!" And when they had cleared the buffet of refreshments, and received all the bounty that the flattered king or count cared to bestow, they went on and did it all over again to a fresh set of victims in the next castle.

And by this time we were over the Rhone, and climbing the steep roads to Villeneuve-les-Avignon, towards the tower and the fortress of Saint André on the crest. In this fortress religious fugitives used to take refuge from the mighty popes of Avignon, at the time of the Great Schism.

As we were not sure where we could lunch, we went down a cobbled street, and pulled up at an odd-looking sign called " Au Chien Blanc." The impressionistic white dog painted on the sign was a rather clever piece of artistry. The proprietress came to the door at our knock, and had a long talk with Rosemary, while we vainly tried to place her odd " dialect," which we took to be local. Then, quite suddenly, when she had given us all the kind information we wanted, and regretted that her own restaurant would not be open for another week, she dashed into rapid English, and Humphrey and Johnny and I, at least, recognized at once that the curious accent of her " dialect " was exactly the same as our own!

She said that the sign had been painted for

her by a friend, quite a well-known artist; but the
natives of Villeneuve-les-Avignon were so horrified
by the eccentricity of this futuristic rendering of a
dog that they came to the conclusion that she was too
poor to afford a better one; and, out of the purest pity,
a neighbourly carpenter offered to paint her a really
good sign, a proper dog with all four legs in place, a
dog that one need not be ashamed of. He would do it
cheap, he said.

She then startled us by asking if we carried revolvers; and when we replied in the negative, retorted:
" Well, you'll need them! " Johnny remarked that he
had thought it was not legal to carry arms in France;
and she gave us the curious piece of information that,
provided the revolver is used *inside* the car, it is legal,
but if outside, then it is against the law. We foresaw
that there might be moments when it would be difficult
to coax would-be robbers and murderers to enter the
Fiat, before shooting them; but, fortunately for our
peace of mind, we quickly forgot her sinister warning,
and never felt our lack of fire-arms very acutely.

We realized that it was a stiff climb to the
fortress which defied the Palace of the Popes from
the top of the hill; and that if we did not do it before

lunch, we were unlikely to do it at all. In fact, through-out the whole of the tour we were constantly in battle against our native sloth. . . . " Especially yours! " added one of my so-called friends, at this juncture; or possibly it was my husband who spoke.

At the Église de la Collegiale, half-way up the hill, I was rewarded for my energy by the display of one of the loveliest little statues I have ever seen — a Madonna and Child, carved in dark ivory from the whole tusk of an elephant. The curve of the tusk was responsible for the happy accident of the Virgin's seeming to lean away from the child, as a mother does in a spontaneous gesture of pride, that she may see him better; or in play with him. The sculptor was a Saracen prisoner, brought to Villeneuve during the crusades. And the guardian of this treasure, a hand-some, melancholy young soldier, wounded from the War, showed us the lovely little image with so much obvious delight in it, so much appreciation of our appreciation, that it was clear that, though the first sight of her took your breath with sudden rapture, yet dwelling with her, seeing her day after day, had crystallized this rapture into a quiet fervour of adora-tion. His passion I could well understand, for I have

THE IVORY MADONNA
AT VILLENEUVE-LES-AVIGNON

never seen, in paint or in marble, a more human, a more tender presentment of the Virgin and Child. I wish you could all see my little ivory Madonna at Villeneuve-les-Avignon; that unknown and possibly unthanked Saracen prisoner left a great gift with his captors.

On the wall of the same room as the niche in which she stands is an exquisite piece of embroidery, a Sacrament veil, a design of the sacred dove in a sacred sun, surrounded in turn by conventional flowers and leaves, the whole worked in tiny seed-pearls.

We left the church regretfully, and clanged the great bell outside the doorway at the end of the left tower, just within the doorway of the mediæval fortress. A troubled, middle-aged woman, whose face had yet retained a quality of fierce dark beauty that reminded me of the Santa Barbara, patron saint of gunners, hanging in the church of Santa Maria Gloriosa dei Frari in Venice, showed us over the tower. My chief memory is of stone walls, six feet thick; of stone walls carved and scribbled over by desperately bored prisoners; and of countless spiral staircases; also a marvellous view, from the roof, across the Rhone to the line of the Palace of the Popes, and the distant landscape of Provence, glittering faintly under sun and mist.

Santa Barbara, noticing Humphrey's leg, charged him only half-price for admittance, saying that this was a law in France for the wounded of every nation, and we would find it in operation at any monument we visited, all over the country; which struck us as a gracious concession on the part of the French. She told us, furthermore, that her husband, too, had lost his leg, but above the knee; and so they had given him the job of guide at this much-visited fortress, where, had he not had a good wife, he would have had to climb spiral staircases all day long. It seemed odd that the thoughtfulness of France should go far enough to provide the wounded with jobs, and not go a little farther, and provide them with the right job.

We had lunch on the shady veranda, arched with vines, of the Restaurant au Printemps. It is not marked in the Michelin Guide; so at first, in utter dependence upon M. Michelin, we took this to mean that we could expect only a meal that we should describe in England as " rough," or " rustic " — in

other words, bread and cheese. What we were given
as a matter of course, was this: hors d'œuvres —
about seven or eight varieties; tunny fish *à l'Italien*,
cooked in a delicious tomato sauce; lobster *brandade*,
the fish prepared in a creamy sort of paste, held in a
patty of light and delicate pastry; pork with spa-
ghetti ("I'm sunk!" said Humphrey, at this juncture. "I am Humphrey the Fourteenth, known as
Petit-Panche!"); cheese-cakes; cream-cheese; melon;
and coffee.

With this meal we drank first vermouth; then
a particularly good red *vin du pays*, with a rose-petal
taste; then a bottle of Tavel; and brandy. The bill for
four of us amounted to ninety-four francs; that is to
say, at the then rate of exchange, roughly eleven
shillings. Everything was of the best bourgeois cooking and serving; one did not compare it with the
chapon fin in Bordeaux, any more than one would
compare an old folk-song with Beethoven. We were
waited on by a pretty girl, keenly interested in our
taste, and in what food pleased us, and our host and
his wife personally superintended the drinks and
chatted with us — but not too much; and oh! the
enormous difference between their discreet geniality

and the type of proprietor who lingers by your table just two minutes too long, when you are tired of being amiable and want to get on with your dinner, and do not dare say: " Get out! "

And when, after lunch, we were shown clean bedrooms with running hot and cold water, wooden floors, and wire mosquito-netting over doors and windows, all the rooms opening on to terraces and the garden, falling down and down to the river, we determined that here would be a good place to stay; a place where " roughing it " need not necessarily mean doing without any comforts, food, or drink!

After lunch we drove to Tavel, through rich vine and olive country, shielded from the mistral by cypress screens planted like a row of soldiers in close formation. In the background a detachment of low cliffs looked as though they should be washed by the sea, instead of by indolent sunlit vegetation. The effect of the Provençal country-side is so lush that it makes you feel at once glowing and lazy, and steeped in soft, bright colours. It makes you feel complacent, as though you had created it all and found it good; and I, personally, was glad that in this it touched my preconceived vision of Provence, and ran for a while side by side with it, before reality branched off again into a different road.

A shepherd, as fat as Mr. Chesterton, with a flock of the thinnest sheep I have ever seen, held up our car for a while. . . . The contrast led one to believe, perhaps mistakenly, that he was not a kind man. But we noted with approval our chauffeur's consideration for live-stock that he met on the road. Our path on that and on every future day was to be continually obstructed by cows that moved slowly, while their round, bewildered eyes rolled sideways towards us; by kids that leapt in a panic; and hens that scuttled for a while to and fro in front of the car, before their understandings led them to make for the other side of the road, while Humphrey slowed up, and roared formidably: " Death to chickens! " By dogs that leapt, barking, at the wheels, and by flocks of sheep that hustled and padded along the middle of the road, their woolly sides rubbed together, while they uttered little bleating, distressed noises. But we killed no live creature on our tour, not the sleepiest, nor the most foolish.

At Tavel we found that the chief wine-grower was a charmingly modest mason, who shyly took us along to his little cellar, where apparently the best

Tavel lay in wood. We each drank a glass of 1924, and we bought a bottle of 1922 to take away with us. That bottle became a curse. Somehow or other it never got drunk, and never got thrown away, so that I cannot tell how good or how bad it was. It survived the tour as far as Bordeaux, and then just vanished. Personally, I like Tavel very much as a light luncheon wine. It has enough body not to be insipid, and it is refreshing without making too many demands on the palate. But perhaps it does not travel well, for I have never met it outside the Rhone locality. They make an eau-de-vie from the Tavel grapes, which, the mason told us proudly, is fifty-five per cent alcohol, and exceedingly fiery.

That night we dined at the Restaurant Lance, driven away from our own hotel by the announcement on the menu, specially underlined for our benefit: "Cod *à l'Anglaise.*" A sentimentalist, no doubt, would have stayed and eaten it; but not for that were we making a study of the cuisine of France. And our epicurean selfishness was rewarded, for at the Lance we were certainly given cod — there must have been a large haul of cod near Avignon that day — but in the form of *brandade* again, and as near perfection as that succulent speciality of Provence can ever hope to be.

Here is the recipe, as near as we can get it, for *brandade:* Boil and bone the cod, and pound it up finely in a pestle. Then place it in a saucepan on the fire, together with two other saucepans, containing milk and olive-oil respectively. Allow all three to simmer gently, and while they do so, add alternate tablespoonfuls of the milk and oil to the fish, stirring in slowly, until it has reached the consistency of a smooth creamy paste. Serve inside little *bouchées* of flaky pastry, or on slices of toast.

Humphrey quite lost his head over *brandade.* He talked of nothing else throughout the rest of our very excellent meal, and was so occupied with telling us at length the effect of *brandade* on his gastronomic psychology that his wine was removed before he had finished it; whereat he broke down, and wept like a little child, and we all said, in the striking phraseology of Mr. Badger to the loquacious Toad, in *The Wind in the Willows:* " *That'*ll learn him! Learn him, learn him, *learn* him! " For the wine was an extremely silky

Châteauneuf du Pape — Château Fortiat 1922, rather more on the Burgundy side than Bordeaux, but with mellow characteristics of its own.

I carried away from the Lance a memory of two delightful pictures: the first was of a large Greek family, who filed into the restaurant while we were there — mother, father, and seven children, all of them beautiful. The last child in the procession noticed that the strap of her sandal was unfastened, and the last child but one stooped and knelt and did it up. The graceful pose, held for a moment in the doorway, was immortal and strangely familiar. . . . Was it on an urn I had seen it before? Or on a frieze? . . . The other picture, of a different era and civilization, was of the proprietor, who looked and talked his part with appreciation of the fact that he should be fat, suave, and tactful; complimentary without losing his dignity; interested, and yet not too intimate; and that he should introduce his patrons to their food and drink, and the food and drink to his patrons, taking as much trouble as M. Balieff presenting his program of the Chauve-Souris to an expectant audience.

They let rooms at the Lance, clean and inex-

pensive, with hot and cold running water in each bedroom. I think thirty francs a night for the largest
room, with two beds, was their charge. At present they
have only one bathroom, but within the next six
months three more are to be added.

After dinner we strolled into the café opposite,
" Au Coq Hardi," attracted by enormous water-colour
paintings on coarse canvas stretched across the walls.
They were signed by an artist named P. Mail. The
subjects were broadly comic, with a suggestion of horror about them, perhaps not intended by the painter.
One, for instance, showed a crowd of good-natured
bourgeoisie, feasting; a flushed dame with her bonnet-
strings knotted, holding her sides and panting with
laughter at the sight of a small boy, lifted on to the
table to display, by his posturings, that he was drunk.
I was reminded, possibly more by my own personal
reaction than by the paintings themselves, of Cruik-
shank, of Hogarth and Rowlandson. But Humphrey
said that they were startlingly similar to the paintings
of Pieter Breughel, for whose work he had a great
enthusiasm.

I was obliged to confess ignorance on the subject of Pieter Breughel and his masterpieces, and I

asked Humphrey to enlighten me. Whereupon I learnt that he was a Dutch artist of the sixteenth century, with a taste for caricature which must have been rather out of place among the artistic schools and conventions of his time. Humphrey's interest in Breughel had first been aroused by two pictures, one in the London National Gallery, the other at Hampton Court. The first is a portrayal of the Adoration of the Magi; the canvas is crowded with figures — kings, shepherds, and Bethlehem onlookers — every one of which is a caricature of a recognizable human type. They are all studies of repulsive abnormality; yet they do, to a strange degree, aim their shafts at humanity as a whole. The picture at Hampton Court shows the burning of a farm, with robbers pursuing and slaying pigs and other animals in flight. There is a duplicate of this picture in a gallery at Vienna, by the same artist; but this time it is entitled " The Slaughter of the Innocents," and the beasts are replaced by children. Thus resourcefully did Pieter Breughel adapt his mocking, individual humour and constrain it to meet the demands and pieties of his age!

When we were back in our bedrooms at the hotel, and the question arose of our route next day,

Humphrey produced his ninety-one maps and his Michelin Guide; and, with that quality of complete and unmannerly absorption which is so characteristically masculine, he and Johnny plunged . . . and did not come up again for the next hour. Now and then, Rosemary and I asked a question. We gathered that we were to be allowed to come along with them, and were mildly interested as to the question of whither and how. Humphrey answered occasionally: " Wait a minute! " Johnny did not answer at all.

And I told Rosemary that the next day I was going to buy a Michelin Guide of my own.

III
"MICH"

THIS is to be a short chapter set apart and dedicated, in profound thankfulness, to M. Michelin, and also to Compagnie, lest Compagnie should be hurt at being left out.

The Guide Michelin is twenty-two years old. It is issued every year, and it costs fifteen francs. If it cost a hundred and fifty francs, I should grumble a little, no doubt, but readily pay it. It contains, perhaps, between two dumpy red covers, more helpfulness, more benignity, accuracy, and compressed information, than any other publication of its kind. Its presiding spirit is a comic little goblin, called by Michelin and Compagnie Bibendum, and made entirely of rubber tires. The Michelin Guide is full of fascinating pictures of Bibendum, showing him either enjoying the advantages of a motor-tour accompanied by the Guide, or else the victim of things no motorist should do. Bibendum is exultant, yet easily depressed, a high-spirited little fellow, winning, by his pranks and capers, even those few people who are not naturally fascinated by guides and maps.

Besides the Guide and the ninety-one maps, covering all the departments of France, we also had our individual route drawn up under the supervision of Michelin. This informed us, not only which roads to take, but whenever it was our bounden duty to raise our eyes and observe a Roman ruin or a fourteenth-century château on the left bank of the Loire; or it mentioned that by going half a kilometre farther than straight on we should pass through scenery that was " *pittoresque,*" on a road that was " *sinueuse.*" . . . One could almost hear him add, with a gallant bow and smile: " *Ça fera plaisir à madame, n'est-ce pas?* "

The entire detailed plan, as well as the Guide, oozed with this desire that we should always be entertained, sometimes profoundly moved — the emotions stirred; that our travelling should be convenient, and that we should not get lost or broken down by the wayside; that we need never rely on our own ignorant

selection of an inn or hotel; in fact, that the whole responsibility of our comfort and our pleasure, even
more than our instruction, was with Michelin, and his
attendant sprite, Bibendum.

As for the Wonder-Guide itself, opening it at
random, under C you find the town of Cambrai, and a
map of Cambrai directing you through the town by
means of figures and letters. You will be told the de-
partment where Cambrai is to be found, the number
of inhabitants, and the altitude. Under "*voir,*" you
will be directed what to see: churches, arches, ruins,
and so forth; the "*spécialités*" are apparently "*bêtises de Cambrai (bonbons).*" . . . I should like to
have tried the *bêtises de Cambrai!* Also "*andouil-
lettes.*" Next you are informed where the library is,
and the Comité d'Initiative, which exists in the smallest French town. Then, really attractively, in the short-
est possible way, you get full information about the
hotels, thus: a five-house hotel, indicating the highest
standards of luxury and expense, is drawn with five
little roofs; followed by the name, the prices of the
meals, the prices of the rooms, and the number of
rooms; C.C. for central heating; and a picture of a
little electric-light bulb to indicate electric light

throughout the house — and this, incidentally, we found in every hotel we stayed at in France, even the one-house; a drawing of two little taps side by side shows hot and cold water laid on in every bedroom; another drawing, primitive but enlightening, tells you how many bathrooms and w.c.'s. The whole of this artistry packs itself into one or two closely printed lines; and all you need do at Cambrai, for instance, is to decide whether you prefer the Hôtel de France, with two bathrooms and twenty-five bedrooms, or the Hôtel du Mouton Blanc *et* Moderne — an irrelevance of association in the title which is very dear to me! — with one bathroom and thirty-five bedrooms. Both of these are one-house hotels. Cambrai also has a two-house hotel, but does not rise beyond that. Also, I made a bad choice when I picked out Cambrai as typical, because Cambrai has no restaurants, and I wanted to tell you all about the stars and the egg-cup and spoon.

Stars are a very dignified business, denoting a high standard of cooking and general style; but we have frequently had an excellent meal where the humility of an egg-cup-and-spoon mark might at first seem discouraging to English people who took these promises literally. Yet I have had five courses, beautifully served, at an inn marked only with an egg-cup and spoon.

There is really no end to the pleasures of Michelin. I have opened it, again at random, to find something which I had not seen before — two golf-clubs crossed, with a little ball, and the number eighteen. . . . It is no good pretending not to know what this indicates. Let us return to Cambrai!

The hotels are followed by a list, with addresses and particulars, of all the garages where you can get Michelin tires. Then about thirty towns are mentioned, with their distance from Cambrai, in kilometres. Cambrai is sixty-five kilometres from Bethune, and a hundred and sixty from Paris.

If ever you are really bored, you could employ several happy hours with Michelin, making a vast calculation of how many hot-water taps exist at the present day in the whole of France, and if all the Hôtels d'Europe et de la Poste were laid side by side with all the Terminus Hotels, which would soonest get to Rheims? — both starting at the same time from Périgueux in Dordogne, . . . where, so Michelin says, it is very difficult to drive your car on a Wednesday through the principal streets, till fourteen o'clock, because of the cattle market. I cannot refrain from burdening you with the further information that the luscious and decadent specialities of Périgueux are truffles, *pâté de foie gras*, and prune brandy. I can vouch for this being correct because I tried all three!

I am terribly afraid that my halting and confused descriptions of the glories of a Michelin Guide, and of the genius and the shining goodwill to men that must have inspired it beyond mere business calculation, have been inadequate, and that readers will say: " Fancy all this fuss about a guide! " There are many poets who have felt the same hopelessness of achievement when they have completed a song-cycle in praise of their love! In Tonnerre (Yonne) there is a fair on the last Saturday of every month, and its specialities are snails and *gougères*. *Gougère* is a *brioche*, made out of Gruyère cheese. Michelin does not like Madame to be puzzled even for a moment, even about *gougère*, the speciality of Tonnerre (Yonne). Michelin would not like her to be inconvenienced by going there on the last Saturday of the month, between eight and seventeen o'clock. I think he must be a very good man. God bless Michelin!

IV
ALPILLES, AND A WILD–BOAR

SO, with two Michelin Guides, ninety-one maps, and our individual Michelin route, we started off the next morning on our tour. Actually, the plan of the week had very little relation to wine, including, as it did, Saint-Remy-de-Provence, Les Baux, Arles, Nîmes, and Orange, little Provençal towns with magical names that have been so often ringed and festooned about and about with descriptive prose and verse and story and legend by other devotees that I will try now to rush through them without lingering. We were at least a week too early for the vintage everywhere; in fact, as it turned out, a fortnight or three weeks too early; for, owing to lack of rain, a late summer, and too much heat when summer actually did come, the gathering was unusually late in the vineyards along the Rhone, as well as in Bordeaux and Burgundy.

And at the moment we were glad of it, for Provence demands a leisurely mood. You should saunter where in other places you run; and sit about for hours, slowly sipping, slowly watching the slow oxen pass, slowly waiting for sunset, and sometimes engaging a slow old Provençal in slow conversation that winds and leads nowhere, except to the city of idle well-being. The very leaves from the plane-trees, when, at rare intervals, one would fall from the branch, spinning and twisting in the soft sunlight, seemed in no haste to reach the ground.

Saint-Remy-de-Provence satisfied us when we arrived, towards evening, after a lunch at dusty Château-Renard, by proving in every way what Johnny had expected Avignon to be. Avignon, with its trams and bustling boulevards in the prosperous portion of the town, had been a great shock to Johnny, who had thought to find one dog, slumbering in one drowsy village street, and the Palais des Papes dreaming, unvisited, behind it.

It was, I believe, of Saint-Remy-de-Provence that Ford Madox Hueffer, one of the greatest modern poets, was thinking when he wrote " On Heaven."

BOUQUET

His idea of heaven was just such another little town in
the valley of the Rhone:

Hard by the castle of God in the Alpilles,
In the eternal stone of the Alpilles,
There's this little old town, walled round by the old, grey
    gardens. . . .

Nothing to do but watch the kindly passers-by; scent
" of cyclamen, of oranges, of rosemary and bay ";
soft, stealing light from the hotel; and always the little
café-tables in the street:

And Arlesiennes with the beautiful faces went by us,
And gipsies and Spanish shepherds, noiseless in sandals of
    straw, sauntered nigh us,
Wearing slouch-hats and old sheepskins, and casting ad-
    miring glances
From dark, foreign eyes at my dear . . .
(And ah, it is Heaven alone, to have her alone and so near!)
So all this world rejoices
In the cool of the even
In Heaven. . . .

. . . Nor does God need to be a very great magician
To give to each man after his heart,
Who knows very well what each man has in his heart:
To let you pass your life in a night-club where they dance,
If that is your idea of Heaven; if you will, in the South
    of France;

If you will, on the turbulent sea; if you will, in the peace
    of the night;
Where you will; how you will. . . .
For God is a good man; God is a kind man;
In the darkness He came walking to our table beneath the
    planes,
And spoke
So kindly to my dear,
With a little joke,
To take away her fear
Of His stature,
So as not to abash her,
In no way at all to dash her new pleasure beneath the planes,
In the cool of the even
In heaven.

— And if I have quoted too much, forgive me; but
this has been for so long a favourite poem of mine;
and so few people have brought it to me, crying enthusiastically: " You *must* read this! " . . . And it
was strange to be actually there, with the Alpilles
close behind, in Saint-Remy-de-Provence, which, if it
was not Ford Madox Hueffer's heaven, was very like
it indeed!

Behind the hotel was a big, lush, untidy Provençal garden, with high walls, and whiffs of tropical
flowers tangled with more familiar fragrances; and
it was full of skipping animals, that slipped away and

reappeared; wild, shy little animals that might have
been striped, or might have been merely striped by the
falling sunlight through the trees, as they rapidly
darted in and out of the thicker shade. And in that
garden we found Taillot; a baby *sanglier* they called
him, which means a wild-boar, captured in the Alpilles, and brought back and tamed.

. . . Taillot, rootling in the undergrowth;
glimpse of a long, narrow head, a long, narrow body
on tall legs, short, harsh yellowish hair. . . . Taillot
butting at a big dog, who surveyed such strange mode
of attack with tolerant surprise. . . . But he would
notice it by and by, when the wild-boar was no longer
a baby. For the benefit of this volume we asked the
proud labourer who had found little Taillot, and who
caught him up now and cuddled him affectionately,
how his name was spelt — " Taillot? Taillaux? . . ."
The man laughed at the question as though we had
asked him something absurd: " *Ça s'écrit comme on
veut!* " he said, which is a method to simplify all
spelling if it could but be universally adopted.

We dined at Saint-Remy, on the open veranda
over the garden, and drank a Châteauneuf du Pape
which tasted like nice chewed grass. This was Rose-

mary's definition, and Johnny and Humphrey said she was right. Personally, I found as little suggestion of chewed grass, even of nice chewed grass, as I had found of rose-petals in Tavel, or of gun-flint in Saint Péray. By this time I was growing humble about my indiscriminating olfactory nerves, and content to accept the verdicts of my friends.

And while we ate and drank in the warm dark, we discussed the roads of France, of which we were having our first experience, and over which we were to travel more than two thousand kilometres before we arrived home again. And we perfected a Wellsian idea of the super-car, which, in five hundred years, would be able to manufacture its own road as it went, pushing it ahead, and laying it down, and running over it, and then picking it up again from behind. It seemed to us a brilliant notion as we evolved it; but perhaps the taste of nice chewed grass was responsible. . . .

What amazed us so especially about the roads in France was their extreme of goodness compared with their extreme of badness, and the way in which neither of these extremes lasted for more than a few kilometres. Sometimes, indeed, a surface composed entirely of holes, bumps, and stones, would alternate about five times in a kilometre with smooth tarmac, soothing to our tortured nerves like a long drink to a thirsty throat.

Now why — this was the way our logic argued it — if they *knew* that this bit of road was so agonizingly bad as to make it so divinely good, why did they leave the next piece unmended, as though they were blind to it, as though it were not there, as though it were none of their business? Nearly always outside every town, after we had been bumped and jolted in a way that caused us to vow that the French should remain unforgiven for ever, we would glide easily on to what we called the " face-saver." Some crafty brain had apparently planned that we should never actually enter a town thinking bitter thoughts; and indeed, so easily swayed were we that, though we recognized the purpose of the " face-saver," yet the motion of our wheels, flying along as though on the track at Brooklands, was so pleasant that we soon began to say: " Ah well, most of the roads are like this! It's only now and then that we come across a bad bit. We mustn't be too hard on them. They are doing their best for us! "

Near Saint-Remy are some Roman remains — a triumphal arch and a tomb, which are supposed to be among the oldest in the country. The wrinkled old guide, with the hooked nose and the fierce beard, who showed — nay, who showed off — the remains, did not lapse from the extraordinarily high and scholarly standard of guides who appear to be selected for such jobs in France. Very contemptuous was he of those tourists who halted there only to ask foolish, flippant questions; and he hauled forth a number of tattered, brown old manuscripts, with illustrations, to prove his point in an argument with Johnny over Roman history. He had fought in the war of 1870; and his father-in-law, so he told us, had died at the age of a hundred and twenty-six. He probably had other claims to distinction, but these were the only ones that we discovered that day.

The triumphal arch stands high, with a glorious view over the surrounding plains of Provence, the silvery shimmer of olives, and the warm kindliness of wild myrtle and aromatic pines; Avignon and the Rhone in the distance; and countless mountains silhouetted sharply in waves, one behind the other, like the great Alps dwindled to miniature. Every feature of big mountain scenery — passes and peaks — we found thus reduced to scale, as we drove on to Les

Baux; and to those who, like myself, love everything about mountains except their aweing immensity, and the horrible necessity of sometimes climbing them, this midget reproduction was as delightful as when, while still a child, and rarely taken to the theatre, you are suddenly given a toy theatre in your own nursery, with full power over its mechanism.

On our way through these Alpille mountains, we passed a curious landscape of low white cliffs, hewn out in blocks and angles, leaving the suggestion that a cave-folk had once lived in this land, and then abandoned it; that the sea had once washed up as far as here, and then withdrawn neglectfully. Actually it was where the soft limestone had been quarried out in great blocks for building-purposes. Yet those white rectangular shapes that met my eye wherever I looked were strikingly familiar. . . . Suddenly, I remembered whose vision it was behind mine, directing it; for here, expressed in scenery, was the essential Nevinson technique.

We saw an eagle on the road to Les Baux. He looked very like a national symbol, as he hovered with taut wings outstretched. Gradually, and nearly imperceptibly, a soaring clump of crags and peaks in the distance merged into the ruins of Les Baux, with three brilliant turquoises set in a grey matrix, where the sky pushed through the jagged holes which had once been the castle windows.

This first visit to Les Baux was in the late afternoon; as we sat on the terrace of the inn, the setting sun poured gold over the broken walls on the ridge above us, and then slowly sucked back all colour except for two flaming quills lying sharply across the pale crocus of the western sky. The honeycombed rocks seemed more than ever habitations of a kingdom that had been punished by desolation. The hills, like cliffs, ghost-white, were washed round by the silvery plain, which every moment grew more and more like the sea. . . . Sea-feeling everywhere, and spectres. . . . And at the little crooked Hostellerie de la Reine Jeanne a sign which stated politely, in English, that the proprietor was late of the Carlton, the Ritz, and the Savoy, which reassured us. So we decided to return home to Saint-Remy, and to lunch at Les Baux the next day.

After our dinner we were persuaded to drink a strange white eau-de-vie, pre-war, called Marc, the name for brandy made from the lees of local wine, rather in the style of Dutch schnapps. Humphrey remarked that it tasted like the drippings from wet leather. I admired the man's versatility in his choice of comparisons.

Johnny, of course, had found a wolf-dog, and was dead to all other interests. . . . Wherever we went, sooner or later on arriving in a village, Johnny would remark: " There's a wolf! " and would hurl himself from the car, or the meal, or his bedroom window, in order to make love to the adorable Alsatian who reminded him of his own Boris at home. Our trail was punctuated by Johnny's " There's a wolf! " And we waited in dread of what, however, fortunately never did happen — that one day he would melt into the arms of a wolf who liked him rather less than he liked it!

V

HIGH HILLS AND HIGH BROWS

THE next morning, September 9th by now, we loaded up our suit-cases and drove to Les Baux again, *en route* for Arles. Before starting off on our explorations of the fortified town, whose ruins were inseparable from the living rock, we drank some vermouth, in excellent company gathered haphazard on the veranda of the Hostellerie de la Reine Jeanne: a French sailor, who had been to New Zealand and Cardiff and other wild places — so he boasted to us; and his wife, who had nursed him during the War, at Havre, and who told me that she had a deep love in her heart for all English, because they were so amiable; the host of the inn, late of the Carlton, the Ritz, and the Savoy — and truly he seemed no less familiar with these way-side pubs than with his own; the guide who was presently going to conduct us over the

ruins, a thoughtful, handsome woman, tanned and
barefooted, wearing a short, ragged black dress; and,
finally, a most seductive little Parisienne, staying at
the inn; an actress, and probably, had we but recognized her, very well known, though she did not
flaunt herself about, but smiled, and kept in the background, and told us, with a pretty bow towards the
host of the inn, that she always returned there for rest
and holidays in September and October, for she knew
of no better place. Had I been a man, I should have
found it easy to rake out some inevitable reason why
I, too, should go to Les Baux in September and October. . . . The incongruous is always charming. Even
from the point of view of a woman I felt a distinct
yearning to stay there in the shade, idly talking to
her, instead of scrambling up in the slippery glare to
where hot crags were lifted in a jagged rim against
a hot blue sky.

I never mind ruins — in fact, I am sometimes
keenly absorbed — once I get among them; but there
is that horrible moment of initiative when your guide
stands ready, and you know it is all to come, and none
of it behind you. And by some silly self-made rule,
wholly breakable and never broken, lunch is for-

bidden until after you have seen the ruins. So we followed our guide up the steep grey street, which may have hummed with life and movement, gaiety, murder, war, and merchandise, in the fourteenth century, but was now dead walls and dead doorways, abandoned to the mistral.

We learnt that Les Baux, when it had been prosperous and the lords of Les Baux had lived there, had been a town of over four thousand inhabitants. " Now," said our guide, " there are no more than thirty, and none of them young." And at this, as though in contradiction, a door was flung violently open, and a flaming lady emerged and rushed violently past us, up the street. . . . We had a glimpse of bright blood-orange hair, hanging down in a tangle beyond her waist, a vividly enamelled face, a demure white and blue muslin frock, and a bottle of wine swung from each hand. Then she disappeared down an alley, and the road was dead again. . . .

The grey buildings, as we climbed higher, became more and more indistinguishable from the rock. They had queer marks on them, where they had been persistently knuckled by the mistral wind; marks unlike the usual rounded swirls by which artists in the style of the late Walter Crane inevitably presented a symbolic suggestion of wind, in their drawings. Mistral had materialized into something less dignified and more fretful, up at Les Baux.

In the church we saw a sort of wheeled chair, in which the lamb and sheep that were sacrificed to the Infant Jesus every Christmas were first taken round from altar to altar, and from house to house, accompanied by the tabor and pipe and old Provençal folk-songs. It ought to have been wheeled round by only youthful devotees, but again our guide shrugged her shoulders, with that ironic, mournful gesture: " There are none, at Les Baux."

The old Roman winepress, hollowed out of one of the thick stone walls, then drew our attention; and hundreds of little hollows scooped regularly in the stone, which she told us were ancient pigeon-cotes. The counts of Les Baux had enjoyed an original " *droit de seigneur* " in the form of " *droit des colombiers* ": from each family of peasants who huddled close under the castle walls for protection against their enemies, had been exacted so many pigeons a year, as a gift to their liege lord.

Many strange fragments of information and

AN OLD ROMAN WINEPRESS AT LES BAUX

wisdom were dropped, as though against her will, by this queer, well-educated woman, with the hips of a peasant, and the deep-set troubled eyes of a creative artist or a philosopher. She laughed with us about "Les Porcelets," the ribald name given to a house where a fourteenth-century count, of peculiar fecundity, had produced over forty offspring, a jest carven immemorially into the stone over the arches. She told us that she had been reading *Ariel* by André Maurois, and thought Shelley was a deeply wronged man, and very nearly a saint: "*Il était adorable, ce Shelley.* I could have forgiven him anything!" And we did not contest the point. And when I, feeling sentimental about the soft, rich, shimmering landscape spread out before us from the battlements, murmured appreciatively: "They call this country '*le pays du tendre,*' do they not?" she replied, with one briskly destructive sentence: "Yes indeed, the country of the soft! They are good, the people of this country, but soft in the head — tender. It is the same thing!"

I try to check the habit, if possible, of making wistful, winsome little vignettes of "characters" whom one meets while wayfaring; but I could not refrain from wondering a little about this guide, her shrouded past, and her problematic present. There was a Scotch quality about her personality and dialogue; I could imagine her living in Edinburgh, and lecturing at the university. . . . Several dry brilliant misogynistic professors would be her intimate friends; and then, suddenly and inexplicably, she would marry a champion golfer, and they would mourn her ever afterwards, saying: " What's become of Waring, since she gave us all the slip? " . . . But meanwhile she guided us down the steep slippery grass, back to the hotel, quietly accepted her tip, and disappeared. We turned our thoughts to lunch.

Lunch, on a crowded veranda overlooking the valley and the Pavilion of the eternal Reine Jeanne, was, gastronomically, a great success; and spiritually we were given such a rare treat that we felt we should never again be ungrateful to chance. The partridges and stuffed tomatoes were delicious. We drank a *vin rosé* with the hors-d'œuvres, which always appear, and are always plentiful; and then went on to Clos des Papes, Châteauneuf du Pape, 1921. I cannot remember that it was not excellent, but later experience taught me that 1921 is a bad year for Châteauneuf du Pape, and that 1920 is the year to aim for, and certainly when ordering Château Rayas or Château Fortiat.

We almost invariably argued during the hors-d'œuvres, which need not be taken too seriously; and only subsided into attentive and intelligent silence when we reached the red wine and the game. So that, from mention of the pretty little Parisian actress, we drifted quite naturally into a fairly open discussion about a wife's psychology towards the women of her husband's past; those whom she owns to admiring, and those whom she professes not to admire at all — " I can understand your finding Sylvia fascinating; she fascinates me, too; but *what* you can ever have seen in Helen . . ." I thrust forward a theory, mainly to draw the others, that we — meaning the eternal wife! — if we were being fundamentally honest, admired Helen a good deal more than we admired Sylvia; so that on the surface we most generously lavished our enthusiasm on the less dangerous of the two. Rosemary did not agree with me. The discussion swerved sideways on to our greater anger when the husband was attracted by a girl who was *common*. . . . Humphrey and Johnny hurled themselves gladly into the fray; up till then we had kept personal experience, metaphorically speaking, under the table, and had been merely generalizing. . . .

Suddenly we became aware of a vibration from the next table, occupied by a young couple. They were listening with shocked attention. Without looking their way we marched along into the gay realms of the luridly personal. No, on second thoughts they were *not* shocked. They were " much too broadminded " to be shocked. They merely thought us awful people. On the arrival of the partridge and the Châteauneuf du Pape we neglected the subject of love and talked coarsely and adoringly about our real passions: food and drink. We saw them settling in their own minds that we were the sort of road-hogs who, in an expensive Rolls-Royce, tore through glorious country like Provence (" but never *seeing* it! ") in a whirl of dust and destruction, thinking only of smashing a speed record and of our lunch to come. " The real spirit of Provence — it doesn't *mean* anything to them. . . ."

Well, *we* had been given our chance. Now *they* were going to show us. They began to talk, frightfully naturally, first to each other, and then to a third, a gaunt dark man from the other end of the veranda

who had strolled across to join them, with the preface:
" Didn't we meet on the boat coming over? "

I have said that the original two were a young
couple. I am not sure. They may have been brother
and sister. On the whole, we were most inclined to
believe that they were " cumrades " giving a rest to
the intellectual side of things, and tramping together
through Provence, in a mood of highbrow fourteenth-
century rusticity. He was fair, with a long, peevish
nose. She had dark hair, bundled up all anyhow, and
she wore a queer, djibbahish blue arrangement over a
cotton blouse, and a long and quite terribly encourage-
home-crafts-and-revive-Merrie-England type of skirt.
They carried knapsacks, and did not mind the weight
a bit. I cannot remember if they actually mentioned
Oxford, or if we merely had the impression that that
was their spiritual home.

We were very happy — but my recollection
of the first few moments of their conversation was
blurred, because Rosemary still thought it more courteous to keep up a pretence of a conversation of our
own, whereas I quite unashamedly wished to let it
lapse. They obviously wanted us to listen and be impressed. . . . When the gaunt man, rather older, with

hollows under his eyes, a very blue chin, and no collar, joined them, Rosemary, too, forgot that she was a lady. He so very obligingly asked the cumrades everything that we had wanted to ask them ourselves. . . .

"You're a schoolmaster, aren't you?" he said to the fair young man, after introducing himself as something or other in the Something-or-other Press (a press with specially-made paper, undoubtedly, and wood-cuts); "by the way, that was my wife whom you saw just now, the one in the red tammy and bare feet, drawing water from the well. I noticed you passing us. You're a schoolmaster, I suppose?"

"As a matter of fact," said the man-cumrade, with modest pride, "I'm a priest. I've just been ordered out to Calcutta. . . ."

The talk meandered a little around holidays, tramping through Provence, the Hostellerie de la Reine Jeanne, and then: "Did you think we were all quite mad, last night?" — casually.

Last night? . . . Oh, kingdom of lost joys! Why had we not been there last night?

"I must confess we *were* curious," laughed

the girl-cumrade; " but then, we're rather mad people ourselves, so . . ."

" You didn't know anybody, of course. Well, to begin with, the man who played the — " (I forget what it was that the man played — a tabor, probably; nothing so popular as the ukulele or the balalaika, nor so commonplace as the piano or violin. It must have been the tabor.) At any rate, the man who had played it, as " produced " now by the gentleman who was in the Something-or-other Press, was obviously a bright star, not only of that mad, mad evening, but also of many other evenings, equally unconventional. He emerged as a rude and weird genius, who invented bicycles, painted Provence in a new and inscrutable fashion, was rather difficult to handle, but was obviously as immensely and colossally worth while to the initiate as Francis Thompson was to the Meynells. There seemed a faint hope that " Moore " might appear presently, and that we should see him in person.

A moment's inattention on my part — a desire for more partridge, probably — lost me the introduction to an anecdote about someone who had lain on a sofa with a heart-attack — " We all thought he was dead! " — and who apparently uprose, afterwards, a changed man. . . . "*Every one* of his habits changed! " So that I cannot be sure whether this was still Moore, or another of those present at the mad impromptu party we had missed.

" Do go on with the personnel! " said the girl-cumrade, getting all excited about it.

And then, suddenly, we heard a remark, devastating in its bitterness, from the group at the table on our other side — rather nice-looking French people, recently arrived: " They are English; *ma foi,* you can see it! — all English! " A wave of the hand ringed into a comprehensive circle the cumrades, the dark man with the pipe and the blue chin, and Rosemary, Humphrey, Johnny, and myself. They thought we were all one party. It was our fault for listening to the other three, as though we belonged to them. By this time they were talking about minor books by minor writers of a minor period, with the air that these were, of course, the only books that could be read, and, thank God, nobody else knew about them. But we were too crest-fallen to enjoy any more, even though Moore, in a pointed yellow beard, a temperamental shirt, and cycling-breeches, had just joined them; also "my wife," in the red tammy and bare feet, and the water-pitcher still carelessly held in her hand.

I give thanks for that group at the table next to us on the veranda at Les Baux. I shall always give thanks for them. They made us very happy. But I do wish the Frenchwoman had not thought that we . . .

VI
RHONE WINES

ARLES and Nîmes and Orange, the next three towns we visited, are so much the three loved children of all those who write passionately and reverently of old Provence, that in this book, which is supposed to be loosely strung along a main theme of wine, I ought sternly to check myself from describing ruins and antiquities and Roman remains, the arena at Arles, the arena and the Temple of Diana at Nîmes, the Roman theatre and great triumphal arch at Orange. This theatre and its adjoining hippodrome are, indeed, among the most beautiful and complete buildings that still stand rooted in ancient history; but still . . .

I will describe, instead, what we ate and drank at Arles, and what we ate and drank at Nîmes, and what we drank and ate at Orange. And if my adherence to the material side of life becomes too much of a strain, I will break away to tell of a breathless few moments between sunset and new moon, when we stood on a bridge of the Rhone, the tall castle of Tarascon high on our left, and looked down, on our right, at Beaucaire, summer palace of King René, the water lapping quietly at its steps. Tarascon, Beaucaire, both names of rounded enchantment. . . . We lingered until the ball of the sun dropped behind the shoulder of the hill of Tarascon, and the opal river was drained of rose and flame; we wished under the new moon. . . . And then returned to our headquarters at Nîmes, not wishing to see Beaucaire or Tarascon again, for fear we might remember them less.

We found excellent cooking at the Hôtel du Nord at Arles; and a very sympathetic *maître d'hôtel*, putting in his counsels when needed, and giving due deference to our individual tastes. Our dinner began with water-melon, hollowed and stuffed with small pieces of ice — very refreshing in those hot evenings of a southern September; then *perdreaux*, with their usual melodious accompaniment of truffles and mushrooms in the gravy; and, served afterwards as a savoury, *petits pois,* with a faint flavour of Indian corn lurking in them. It was our habit, whenever possible, to begin the meal by drinking a *vin du pays,* to give ourselves some idea of what it was like. At Arles the *vin du pays* was good and dry, a white wine, which, on the waiter's advice, we followed up with a Côte Rôtie, from the vineyard which we saw many weeks later, on our way back, at Ampuis, north of Avignon. It is a quite good Rhone wine, more like Bordeaux than Burgundy; and this was a 1918, bottled at Saint-Péray, the flavour improving with the cheese: Brie, I believe, and *la navette* biscuits, a speciality of Provence.

We were so pleased with our dinner that we lunched at the hotel again on the following day, and drank an even better *vin du pays,* a red St. George *vieux* — Xavier Perrier of Frontignon, Herault. I am giving the name of the maker, and where it can be procured, for those who would like to add to their cellars a cheap light wine, that is not Chablis nor Montrachet; and which goes well with the opening courses of an unpretentious meal. The *fine* at the end of our meal was a four-star Armagnac, very green and strong.

In Arles, once, a great protectress of cats must have dwelt; for all the picturesque steep streets and alleys are closely inhabited by well-fed, handsome cats; not hungry prowlers, but cats that blink at you sleekly as you pass. This is to Arles's credit. There was one special cat, with queer, black, lynx markings, who would have nothing to say to our advances, but haughtily retired into the Roman theatre. The cat impressed me far more deeply than the theatre itself, which, with its litter of marble and stone and fallen blocks of every sort and size, reminded me of nothing so much as a stone-mason's back yard; but the ancestors of the lynx cat might well have been among the wild animals that were set loose to crunch martyrs in the sunny, blistered arena. In one corner of it Johnny discovered, with sudden excitement, the print of a bull's foot; and the town was hung with posters, enthusiastically announcing a bull-fight on the following Saturday — " *A la mort!* " said the posters, further to tempt sightseers; but I did not know, and did not like to ask, whose death they flourished with such triumphant certainty beforehand: the bull's? or the horse's? or the matador's? And again a passage from " On Heaven " drifted into memory:

Now that *affiche*, in orange, on the kiosque:
" Seven Spanish bulls will fight on Sunday next
At Arles, in the arena." . . .

I liked Arles, and the Hôtel du Nord at Arles;
for I was given a bedroom with the announcement
over the mantelpiece that Napoleon III had slept for
one night in that room; and I am sure he felt as
I did about the pleasure of waking in the morning,
with the green sun-slashed plane-trees of the square
level with your eyes, and in your ears the rhythmic,
patient stamping of horses outside the café below, and
the sound of buckets of water sluicing the pavement;
he must have gone away in a very good temper, first
writing in the visitors' book: " Always pleased to
return and recommend. N."

The road from Arles to Nîmes changed entirely in character from the wild strange scenery of
the Alpilles, which had been with us so far. It was rich
and pastoral; purple loosestrife grew in the ditches.
The flat vineyards, loaded with small blue grapes,
ran parallel on either side; and more vineyards lay
aslant on the distant slopes. We travelled over long,
white, dipping roads, lined with plane-trees, that at
regular intervals sliced the glittering dust with fat

shadows. And we saw our first group of *vendangeurs,* incredibly picturesque women in coloured sun-bonnets, and men in red shirts, and pretty, dark, laughing girls, picking grapes and carting them in hods to the painted cart near by. Not all the modernists in the world, who deify natural ugliness, angularities, elevator buildings, and dung-heaps, can persuade me that it is contemptible to enjoy the sight of a good-looking family picking grapes, in a sunny vineyard of Provence; especially when the oblique evening sun is adding its traditional benison on the day's fruitfulness.

We overtook and passed several carts loaded with grapes and grape-pickers on their way home. They waved their hands to us, and called aloud some greeting, and we replied with: " Hurray for Bacchus! " or something equally appropriate to the spirit of the hour.

I pointed out one cart to Humphrey in which father, mother, auntie, uncle, son-in-law, and about fourteen children of all sizes flopped sleepily over the brim, in the same way as the piled-up grapes lolled over the edge of the baskets. " Look! " I said, " Father made them *all* come out to pick — not even little Humphrey was allowed to remain at home! " And indeed, the little Humphrey of the family was conspicuous by his air of suppressed rage.

" But he complained the most! "

" And did the least work! "

" And felt the most tired! "

" And ate the best grapes! "

Alternately we were filling in the picture of little Humphrey.

— " And reminded them *without* stopping, of what an ill-used little Humphrey he was, and how *well* he was bearing it! "

We went to a three-house hotel at Nîmes, though we avoided three-house hotels whenever possible, as they usually had not the glorious and complete luxury of four- or five-house hotels, and not the intimate comfort and simplicity and welcoming atmosphere of a two-house or one-house hotel.

But at this particular hotel at Nîmes, selected at random, we were to drink one of the most notable wines of our career as amateur connoisseurs — a red Hermitage, 1906, from the firm of Labeaume, Alboussières, Berne et Cie, Saint-Péray. It might have been an even more epoch-making moment in our lives had

it been served to us by a *sommelier* who realized that
good wine should be treated, in the cradle, with the
tenderness due to the seven months' heir of a great
house, where no more are possible. But this wine-
waiter, like so many others of his profession in France,
treated the Hermitage, 1906, as though he were wield-
ing Indian clubs in the gymnasium. His motto was obviously: " The hand that rocks the cradle rules the
world! " Severely, we nicknamed him " Swingbottle "
on the spot, and tasted the Hermitage with very little
hope, though it was our first on the tour. Johnny and
I had once tasted a very inferior Hermitage in some
hotel on the French Riviera.

But this was transcendental. The gun-flint backwash was there, and all the other little subtle flavours
that run up, one behind the other, elusively blending
and disappearing again. For this is the peculiar excitement of a true Hermitage, that you have not yet
done with it when you have relished the bouquet, and
the rich flavour, and the silky texture, and the sight
of its deep clear gold-and-red, shiningly blended. All
these are straightforward appeals, but afterwards
comes the fascination. You follow up your sensations
with the thrill of a hunter after some live creature, with

a will and personality of its own, whom he would catch and tame and bring home. But it is no good; you cannot catch the wild charm of Hermitage, though you drink it and drink it again. You can only marvel at it gratefully.

And the very next day we had the same good luck at the Restaurant Durand at Nîmes, with a white Hermitage this time; 1922, a wine which in theory is too youthful to be drunk with exquisite pleasure; only, on this occasion, practice contradicted the theory. The bottle was from the same firm as the 1906 red, of the night before. So potent was the spell of the wine, in each case, that I took no note of what we ate at either meal, though it is usually safe to say that good drink and good cuisine walked hand in hand, unerringly mated.

Over my bed in the hotel was a printed notice, in English, as follows: " Ring one time for the footman; two time for the chambermaid; three time for the governess."

I speculated, fascinated, on the personality of the " governess," longing and yet fearing to materialize her.

At last, with trembling hands, but with my awe

overcome by curiosity, I stretched up my hand, hesitated, and rang — one time — two time — *three time!*

It was done now, and I must take the consequences. . . .

A loud crash, and a peal of thunder! The walls of space and time wavered, shook, fell apart and joined again. . . . And there she stood — the dreaded governess, dressed in black, tight mouth, hair screwed back, snapping eyes behind gold-rimmed pince-nez.

" Well? " she barked; and I faltered: " *Bail, corail, émail, soupirail* — " and came to a dead halt. It was no good, I could *not* remember. I knew they were exceptions, but what were they exceptions to? Did they take -s or -aux in the plural?

" Well, come along, quickly now! " shrilled the angry governess. She approached the bed, nearer and nearer. . . . What was she going to do? *Bail, corail, émail. . . ?*

" — take the dative! " I screamed, knowing well I was wrong.

The thunder pealed again . . . the vision faded. The room was empty. The governess, suggested by that placard above my head, had been conjured up by my fevered imagination and a bottle of 1906 Hermitage; she was only a memory of Jean Cadell's representation of the dreadful governess in A. A. Milne's *When We Were Very Young.* . . . I had *not* rung the bell three time!

The next morning, on our way to Orange, we stopped for a few moments to look at the great Roman aqueduct, Pont-du-Gard, and its dignified grey arches, in three diminishing tiers, one above the other, spanning the River Gard. It was built in the reign of Augustus, to carry water to Nîmes.

The road ambled pleasantly between Provençal farm-houses, with their deep roofs; glimpses of little towered châteaux, and quince-trees, whose fruit shone genially in the sunshine. At one point, for about a quarter of an hour, whiffs of lavender ran alongside of us, from a plantation on either side. At the crest of a grey village, uphill street, empty and shadowed, I saw baskets of flaming tomatoes and purple *aubergines,* piled up in brilliant profusion, and gaining a yet more startling hue than their own by a sudden sloping sun-ray squeezed down on them between the grey walls. If impressionism had arranged a theatrical *décor,* it could have done no better than to imitate this.

Orange broadened out into the typical *place* of three-cornered bare earth or gravel, and evening skittles played under the plane-trees; the equivalent of our English cricket on the green. The little tables outside the cafés round the triangle were crowded with convivial villagers, basking and drinking and gossiping. A party of zouaves in uniform strolled in and out; and conscripts in dull blue, and old women wearing their local head-dresses. The air of leisure and festivity suggested that it was a Sunday, which is a day of pleasure, abroad.

I have promised to say nothing about the Roman theatre, but I should like to cheat myself by slipping in one memory of that glorious clump of pink and white oleanders, lavishly entangled with a quince-tree, which flourished in one corner of the deserted semi-circular arena; and of the doves that never ceased their soft, triumphal cooing in the after-sunset glamour.

We stayed the night at Orange; and drank, at dinner, first Camp Romain, a pleasant dry white wine, and then Côte du Rhône, 1919, and labelled " Hôtel des Princes et de la Poste "; it was a queer bright rose-colour, with a much stronger effect than had appeared at first taste. The slight bouquet improved all through the meal, and there was a distinct and pleasant backwash. I wonder whether these minor Rhone wines are really spoilt by travel, or whether they simply do not figure on any list, except in their own locality, because nobody ever asks for them.

VII
CHÂTEAUNEUF DU PAPE

AT Châteauneuf-du-Pape we ran into the fair which apparently extends all over the southern parts of France for a fortnight, at this time of year. We went straight to the Hôtel Bellevue, which is marked in Michelin with a star; and were warmly welcomed by the proprietor, a big dark merry-faced man, who, as soon as we explained that we were interested in wine from an intellectual, academic, and literary point of view — we did not put it like that, certainly! — became our enthusiastic ally, and conducted us at once up the road towards the cellars of his friend and patron, M. Prosper Quiot, the proprietor of Clos St. Pierre.

We met M. Quiot himself coming towards us, a genial-looking buccaneer, with grey mustachios, and hat rakishly worn on one side. We had nothing to complain of in his treatment of us; and his pride in his establishment was well justified: all the bottle-cleaning-, labelling-, and corking-machines, which we saw first in actual performance, were extremely up-to-date and hygienic affairs. Six hundred bottles, M. Quiot told us, could by this process be cleaned by one man in an hour. Then we saw the oak casks where the wine was kept for three years in wood, before bottling. Châteauneuf du Pape is apparently a wine which will keep for a long time. M. Quiot still had some 1847. In Italy you are frequently assured that a bottle of wine is " *molto vecchio!* " — very old — " it has already been made six months! "

The best recent years for Châteauneuf du Pape were 1904, 1911, 1918, and 1922. 1921 was a bad year, yet in Bordeaux and Burgundy 1921 is starred as *la Grande Année.*

M. Quiot and his son showed us their vineyards — sandy, very stony soil, more stones than soil. The vines were kept short, but not trained, and would last about a hundred years. Then came the excellent moment when M. Quiot hospitably called for glasses and a bottle of 1920, which was strong in alcohol, with a beautiful bouquet and mellow after-taste, round and soft on the palate, worthy to rank with a good Burgundy.

"But naturally! for Burgundy is made with our good Rhone wines, and mostly with Châteauneuf du Pape," said M. Quiot, when we remarked on this.

"*Tiens?*" exclaimed Rosemary.

Rosemary's "*Tiens?*" was a ripple; a gentle little refrain, questioning and yet full of wide-eyed, acceptance, sounded at intervals throughout our tour of the vineyards of France. She said: "*Tiens?*" when M. Quiot told us that all really good Burgundies were made from Rhone wines; she said: "*Tiens?*" when a proprietor, who shall be nameless, told us that a proprietor, who shall be still more nameless, was a charlatan; she said: "*Tiens?*" when they told us in Bordeaux that the wines of Burgundy were heavy, and tasted of the cooked grape; she said: "*Tiens?*" when a wine-merchant of Pommard told us that real vinous delicacy, subtlety, and flavour were only to be found in Pommard, and not in the vineyards on the Côtes de Nuits — Romanée-Conti, Richebourg, Clos de Vougeot, and so forth; she said: "*Tiens?*" when at Romanée-Conti they informed us that Bordeaux was a *vin ordinaire*, and that Pommard did not exist; she

said: " *Tiens?* " with an inflection of the strongest belief and trustfulness and how-wrong-I-was when a hotel
proprietor, who had nothing in his cellars older than
1919, told us that nowadays real connoisseurs judged
that wine should not be left in the cellar longer than
seven or eight years. I learnt to love the monosyllable
as Rosemary brought it out.

But in M. Quiot's pronouncement lurked a
good deal of genuine truth. As for some peculiar reason there was very little demand for Rhone wines,
compared with Burgundies, for a great many years,
the former had indeed been used to fortify Burgundy,
probably no one being the worse for this arrangement.
But lately the proprietors of vineyards in the Rhone
district are trying to restore to Hermitage and Châteauneuf du Pape some of the ancient prestige and
dignity which they deserve.

Believing quite rightly that wine and food
should go together, M. Quiot told us that his friend the
proprietor of the Bellevue could be trusted to provide
us with the most noble of wines, and that he could
confidently leave the affair to him; and they bowed
to each other, and indicated each other's excellences,
like dramatist and manager taking a first-night call

before the curtain. And, indeed, we were not disappointed in our lunch on the shady veranda at the Bellevue, overhanging the vineyards of Châteauneuf-du-Pape. To begin with, the atmosphere provoked an appetite in itself; lunch was treated as though it were something important, a successful collaboration between the host, the chef, and the lunchers.

We began with a *pâté de lièvre*, which I have eaten nowhere else, cuddled in red jelly; a most soul-satisfying dish. Then river crayfish, *écrevisses à l'Américain*, beautifully served in a flaming Cognac sauce, with little scarlet portions of *écrevisse*-shell built up in the form of red devils, jauntily surmounting the dish; then *perdreaux rôtis* — and does one ever come to the point of saying: " I'm tired of partridge "? However, these were the first we had had, in France, which were high enough. Undoubtedly hills should be low, and game high. *Aubergines farcies* were succeeded by a good Roquefort cheese, the best cheese of all for bringing out the flavour of accompanying wine; and a *fine de la maison*, poured from an oak bottle, bound in brass.

The wines were a white Châteauneuf du Pape, 1922, meriting the highest praise; and then a red of

1911, meriting even higher praise than the highest. Both, of course, were from the cellars of M. Quiot; and he presently came along to join us at coffee, bringing with him souvenirs and gifts, in the form of sample bottles of Châteauneuf du Pape, and playthings that were hollowed corks with dice contained inside. There is nothing like an unexpected present for raising the spirits, and we all parted thoroughly well pleased with each other. We were quite determined to lay down a fair amount of this good Rhone wine in our own cellar.

Before finally departing, the host of the Bellevue took us round the inn, and showed us his relics of the past. His past, surprisingly, was that of a music-hall dancer — mostly patter-dancing, I should say, to judge from the numerous photographs of himself and his wife. We had noticed a slim good-looking woman, with cropped black hair, enormous eyes, and greater agility than belonged usually to the wives of French hotel-keepers, darting and skipping from room to room, active as a lizard, helping with everything, during lunch. She had been his dancing-partner; and here they were, photographed together; and here again, bowing to the audience; and here an enlargement; and here again, he, top-hat in hand, following her short frilly skirts, one toe pointed. The most successful scenes of their career, he told us, had been in Egypt, and one of the relics, proudly exhibited, was somehow connected with the Sirdar: " Your Lor' Kichenaire," but I forget exactly how Kitchener's life had been looped in with those of our friends, the Hôtel Bellevue couple. It is certain that they have a prosperous career ahead of them, as well as behind; for they know their job, and delight in it, exhibiting none of the faint re-sentment and contempt that we should want to eat at all, which I have several times encountered at the same class of hotel in England.

We had a beautiful drive along the east bank of the Rhone, ending with the romantic thrill of seeing in front of us the most famous vineyards in the whole history and kingdom of wine — the hill of Hermitage.

VIII
ANCIENT HERMITAGE

S *I oncques passez en Tournon, vous conseillons bonnes gens, en bons servateurs d'aultruy, vous arrouser de ce jus céleste, car n'est poinct aultre chose ce vin de l'Hermite que rosée paradisiaque, et si vous estonnez de cette diction, oyez la très véridicque et édifiante histoire que nous compta après boyre feu de bonne mémoire frère Jehan Pelefigue, prieur des Capucins.*

Du temps où barbares empereurs de Rome donnaient en pasture aux bestes Christians, un sainct homme de Turnonus s'estant nouvellement converti à la foy de notre saincte Église, pour se soustraire aux soubdars romains lesquels férocement pourchassaient confesseurs de l'évangélicque vérité, se fict un asyle sur l'aultre rivage du Rhosne, en la montagne où l'on voit aujourd'hui belle ordonnance de seps, pères de gros savoureux raisins, pour lors horrificque habitacle de bestes maléficques et vénéneuses. Mais aussi tost incontinent sa venue feurent tous ces animaux non malfaisants, mais amys du sainct homme. Loups doulx

comme agneaux et renarts fidèles comme chiens s'en ve-
naient le soir portant à l'hermite pains et fromages pris es
maistairies. Adoncques trouvait bien à manger mais point à
boyre le pauvret, car n'osait, de paour d'estre prins, descen-
dre au fleuve, pour sa soif estancher, comme faisoient bestes,
au soleil couchant.

Et alloit mourir de male mort, si le très miséricor-
dieux bon Dieu, pour calmer souffrance de son féal subject,
n'avoit envoyé de nuict une troupe de vignerons qui sont
très tous en Paradis (où oncques ne sont allés meschants
beuveurs d'eau) et d'anges complanter de vignes séra-
phicques la retraicte du sainct pour que, si au moins ne
beuvoit d'eau le pauvre, peut au moins boyre du vin.

En effet dans une nuict fuerent meurs à poinct les
raisins pour estre mis en cave, ce à quoy ne faillit l'Hermite
et beut louant Dieu toute sa vie qui dura jusqu'à sa mort.
(Chronicques Vivaroises du F. Benedictus)

In the days when the barbarous emperors of Rome
used to give Christians to the beasts for food, a holy man of
Tournon, being newly converted to the faith of our holy
Church, in order to save himself from the said Romans, who
were fiercely pursuing confessors of the gospel truth, took
refuge on the opposite bank of the Rhone, on the mountain
where nowadays one sees beautiful rows of vines, parents
of great luscious grapes, but which in those days was the
terrible dwelling-place of wicked and venomous beasts. But
immediately on his arrival, these animals became no longer

wicked, but the friends of the holy man: wolves gentle as lambs, and foxes faithful as dogs, came to him in the evening, bringing the hermit bread and cheese taken from the tradesmen. Wherefore the poor man found plenty to eat, but nothing to drink, for he dared not, for fear of being captured, go down to the river to quench his thirst, as the beasts did, at sunset.

And he was about to die a sad death, had not God, in His great mercy and goodness, to allay the suffering of His faithful subject, sent at night a troop of vine-growers, all of whom are in paradise (where, however, impious drinkers of water did not go) and of angels, to plant the retreat of the saint with seraphic vines, so that, if the poor man could not drink water, he could at least drink wine.

And in one night the grapes were ripe enough to be put in the cellar, which the hermit did not fail to do, and drank, praising God all his life, which lasted until his death.

This picturesque legend, which I have translated very roughly, as to the origin of Hermitage, was contained in a leaflet provided by Délas Frères, at Tournon-sur-Rhône; they were among the few proprietors of vineyards on this famous hill, which seems to collect and absorb all the sunshine of southern France. To me, and I do not think I am solitary in this emotion, a special nobility has always draped itself about the very name of Hermitage. It is like a king who has worn a crown and lost it, but never lost his dignity or his faithful adherents. Yes, it is a wine even more imperial than Imperial Tokay, because it is lonelier, and less ostentatiously and magnificently romantic. Imperial Tokay — you roll it on your tongue, with a vision of royalty in gold and purple sitting at a banquet; but Hermitage — and the only picture is of a quiet hill, its steep side facing west; and on the crest, the grey ruins of a shrine.

Yet Hermitage had an immense reputation in England, before the dreadful years of the phylloxera, that devastating germ which, from 1865 onwards, attacked, with very few exceptions, all the old vines of France, of Gaul, and of the Romans; attacked and destroyed them. After that desolation, vines had to be grafted on American stocks, and though Bordeaux and Burgundy regained their popularity, proud Hermitage remained almost forgotten, and underwent the humiliation of being used to strengthen Burgundy and sold under an alien label. But now, slowly, the kingdom of Hermitage is being restored.

We visited the cellars and, later on, the steep vineyards of M. Chapoutier, a charming, courteous

gentleman, with a grey beard, and much of the courtesy and hospitality towards strangers which, in the
Middle Ages, would have associated itself with a
velvet robe, and the gift of a queen's signet-ring. He
told us that the best years of Hermitage were 1904,
1906, 1911, 1915, 1918, 1919, and 1920. It could
safely be laid down for thirty or forty years before the
phylloxera, but now it should be drunk after twenty-
five years. It is kept five years in the wood before being
bottled, unlike most wines, which are kept only three.
To our amazement, M. Chapoutier told us what was
afterwards corroborated by other proprietors and
merchants, that the modern taste is for younger wines,
even when offered a choice. This impatience is ex-
traordinary, for Hermitage is undoubtedly too rough
when young.

Down in the cellars, led by a man with a torch,
the atmosphere was dim and reverent. The walls, and
indeed the barrels, were covered with a soft black
fungus, caused by the evaporation of the wine; the
swathing of fungus and cobweb was never removed,
as it helped to preserve the liquid at an even temperature. It was difficult to believe that we were not
passing through the scene which always precedes the

THE HILL OF HERMITAGE

THE VINEYARDS OF MONSIEUR CHAPOUTIER

transformation-scene at a Christmas pantomime, expensively produced; all the properties and lighting were in order. . . . Presently the one ghostly torch, which flung eccentric shadows on the walls and the vaulted ceiling, would spring into coloured radiance and a thousand lights; and from all the barrels the wine-fairies would trip, and dance against a background of iridescent cobwebs, chasing away the squatting goblins that peeped from round the fungus!

However, none of these events occurred; and M. Chapoutier, the magician in charge, restrained his powers, and contented himself with giving us useful information. Presently, indeed, he was to give us something better! Meanwhile, we saw the stacked-up bottles, and learnt that greenish glass was used for red wine, and yellowish glass for white. The red wine is not pressed at all, but is left for a month in vats, which are then drained; but the white and the rose wines go into the presses.

"And now," said M. Chapoutier, benevolently, " you will do me the honour of tasting my wine? " We did him the honour. Really, the obligations involved on a wine-tour are most attractive! He began by handing round a 1920 red Hermitage. See-

ing us hesitate before uttering a flow of smooth compliments, he begged for the truth. We confessed that,
though good, it was much too young and fiery for our
taste. He seemed pleased that we had not suffered
from the fashion of our generation — or perhaps the
truth is that we are already middle-aged?

In these post-phylloxera days I myself would
put twenty years as a good age to begin drinking red
Hermitage; the white can be drunk with pleasure
earlier. With age the red attains a dark velvety purple
hue; it needs very careful handling, as it throws a
heavy sediment; the white ages to a brownish-gold,
almost the colour of Madeira. Thus matured, each is
far too big to be anything but the principal wine of a
meal. To drink a white Hermitage with your fish, and
to follow it up with a red, would be too sumptuous,
too overpoweringly magnificent, for any one meal.

A 1911 Côte Rôtie followed the Hermitage;
smoother and finer certainly, but of quite different
bouquet; I personally did not rave about it. Then
came a brandy, made from Hermitage grapes; but
first, when he tapped the cask, M. Chapoutier told us
to bend down and smell it. Without exaggerating, the
strength and power which sent me reeling backwards

was like a blow from a man's fist; so we took no more than a sip each of *fine* Hermitage. It was extraordinarily fragrant and exciting, but entirely different from the real brandy that we were accustomed to.

Our host then beckoned his head cellar-man aside, and gave an order for something to be brought to his private office — we could not hear what, but sensed a hushed and significant happening in the near future. And now again the reality of our wine-tour touched and mingled with my fantastic dream of how it might be; for M. Chapoutier, alone of all the many gentlemen who were so kind and helpful to us, opened a bottle of really old wine from his private cellar, an 1874 white Hermitage. Five years it had lain in the wood, and forty-seven in the bottle, and now the supreme hour had come in the life of a heroic wine — not that even my sentimentality could suppose that the hour was as supreme for the wine as for us. It was indeed a very glorious drink; glowing brownish-gold in colour, and with all the subtle characteristics of Hermitage blending in it, gun-flint aroma, and the hunt and chase and capture of the elusive after-taste. We drank M. Chapoutier's health; with a sincere desire, behind the usual empty formality, that such a good and generous man might live fourscore or even fivescore years and ten, and enjoy prosperity and happiness. And then, on an agreement to visit his actual vineyard next day, we parted; but first he gave very precise directions about our future wines, to the innkeeper of our Hôtel de l'Hermitage, who had accompanied us this morning to introduce us to M. Chapoutier.

It was an excellent little inn. We had arrived there the night before, and had already appreciated the dinner. Humphrey and Rosemary knew it of old, and had promised us a very special dish, called " *perdreaux flambés* "; but on our arrival they had not recognized the proprietress, and the thin brisk Madame who took our orders for dinner seemed extremely upset when we insisted on this *flambé.* " *Ah non, non, non, non, NON!* " . . . But why? To this hour we have not understood her reason for so sensitive a complex on the subject.

We began with very small, but succulent melons, a deep apricot tint inside, a speciality of that part of the country. Then we were served with exquisite river-trout, like white-fleshed little princesses. With these we drank a white Hermitage of 1915. It was over-iced, and so had lost some of its flavour, and it struck us as not so good as the 1922 we had already sampled at Nîmes.

After the trout, Madame suggested, with a crafty air, that we had better precede the *perdreau flambé* by chicken; but chicken *and* partridge struck us as gastronomical tautology, and all except Johnny refused it. Johnny, who is perhaps the most carelessly extravagant individual within my knowledge, is possessed by a rigid sense of economy in two or three unexpected and usually inconvenient spots. For instance, he never allows me to use my electric torch, however black the night. I may carry it, but not use it. If I switch it on for a bare half-second, I hear his shocked voice saying: " Put it out! You're wasting it! " . . . Refills cost about ninepence each.

But another of his economies, much more relevant to our journeyings, was his refusal ever to leave a drop in the bottle, or a speck of food on the plate. Fortunately, his nickname was " Brass-belly "!

The partridge arrived, robed in blue flame, but soaked in just a shade too much brandy. We drank a red Hermitage de la Maison with this, 1915, rather too young. This was before our visit to M. Chapoutier, and we were still thinking regretfully of our 1906 from Labeaume, Alboussières, Berne et Cie, Saint-Péray.

But at lunch the next day, after our visit to the cellars, we were consoled by a 1911 white Hermitage (Chapoutier et Cie), beautifully soft, gun-flint flavour not too pronounced, and the colour like lucent sunshine distilled through an autumn leaf. And in the evening we were still more consoled by seeing the magic symbols 1874 again, upon the label of a Château Grillet this time, silky as poppy petals, with a marvellous new witchery in its flavour; so that I felt like saying haughtily, when offered wine in the future, that I never drank anything of less than fifty-two years' maturity!

We had trout again for dinner that night, with the Château Grillet, and some excellent home-cured ham, tender fillets of veal, and real *soufflé* potatoes, with the right amount of air ballooning inside them.

Johnny went alone the next day to keep his appointment with M. Chapoutier; for although we were near the end of September, the golden heat of Provence was soaking and stewing all the energy out of Rosemary and myself. He came back with a great deal of information about the famous *petit syrah* grape, used for Hermitage, except for a white grape called *roussette*, for white Hermitage. Apparently grapes from three parts of the hill are used, one for giving body, one bouquet, and one fineness, and they grow up the hill in layers, top, middle, and bottom. The grapes from each are mixed to make the great wines, but all are the syrah variety. The earth is limy and very stony and shallow, and the grape-vines are dug up and root-pruned every fifteen or twenty years. All this from Johnny's note-book — for he has a passion for accurate horticultural information, that I admire but do not share.

That afternoon he and I visited Délas Frères, to whom we had an introduction. Their premises were in the little town of Tournon, on the opposite side of the bridge from Tain. We were directed to a courtyard with barrels standing outside, and were pleasantly received, first by a workman, then by a manager, and then by the young proprietor, who seemed, however, to be puzzled by our interest in his establishment. After we had gone up and down several rough ladders, and smelt strange smells and seen liquids in a rather new form of vat being stirred, or steamed, or

being otherwise treated in some way of raw materials
that, to the uninitiated, is always equally mysterious,
we discovered that we were in a tannery! And apologizing to the bewildered young proprietor, we re-
treated quickly. . . . And presently found M. Délas
and his nephew, who received us kindly, and gave us
some 1920 red Hermitage, very good, but new. It is
odd to compare this year of Hermitage with the same
year of Châteauneuf du Pape, which we had drunk,
and were to drink again, without feeling at all that it
should have waited another fifteen or twenty years
before being opened. Hermitage *must* be old, which
is probably why so many people have been disappointed in their first experience of it.

M. Délas senior promised us his shy and rosy
nephew as an escort on to the Hermitage hill the next
day, at one o'clock, just before we planned to leave
Tain. He arrived, poor boy, during the latter end of
our lunch, in a state of bashful prostration so extreme
that we, pitying him, caught the infection, and were
likewise nervous and bashful. We came to the conclusion, wrongly perhaps, that he had only just left his
gymnase, and been taken into the business; and that
his uncle had said to him, firmly: "Now see, *mon*

enfant, here is your chance to win for the business *un peu de réclame.* These are influential English." " Ah, *mon oncle, need* I go? " " Certainly you will go. You have a good figure, good clothes! *Mon Dieu,* can you not do something for the firm at last? Go, and cover yourself with glory! " " Ah, *mon oncle,* I shall not know what to say! " " To say? To say? To *say? . . .*" And here the uncle would explode into mere splutterings of " *Imbécile!* " and " *Crétin!* " And poor Armand Gaston Hercule would realize the sickening truth that he must indeed conquer his shyness and go forth to meet those terrifying English.

But hearing that we had never tasted the Mousseux wine of the Côte du Rhône, he generously insisted on ordering a bottle for our dessert. We could not offend him by confessing that we loathed and despised all sparkling wines, except perhaps the very best and dryest Champagne. However, the Saint-Péray Mousseux, though sweet, had a distinct flavour of grapes, and was altogether not quite so awful as we expected. This, however, was not the form in which we praised it to M. Délas junior.

Once we were actually on the hillside of Hermitage, in his own vineyards, he became a little happier; and, in his youthful gallantry, gathered so many bunches of grapes for Rosemary and myself that we imagined the Délas *cuvée* of 1926 was thereby greatly reduced.

The golden, silky heat which lay over the hill of Hermitage, was the very same aroma, rounded, golden, silky, transcending all others, which one tastes in the wine — and which men prosaically call " gun-flint."

IX
ACROSS FRANCE

I T was after we had strapped our suit-cases on to
the car at Tain-l'Hermitage and made a formal
start on our four days' journey across France to Bordeaux that Rosemary and I discovered in each other,
to our mutual satisfaction, a queer reluctance ever to
drink wine again. We spoke with enthusiasm of waters
labelled Vichy, Évian-les-Bains, Vitel, Perrier, Con-
trexeville; and wondered whether it would be possible, from now onwards, to divert the object of our
tour, and make of it a pilgrimage to some of these
spots where mineral waters sparkle, and such tiresome trifles as aroma, body, velvet, and after-taste
need not be considered.

Humphrey and Johnny, however, still had peculiar hankerings for Bordeaux and Burgundy, so
that Rosemary and I could only hope that during our

four days' reprieve, before we should arrive at Cognac, we might regain a little of our original zest. Yet
we philosophized wearily on how soon satisfaction
wraps itself like an opaque blanket round the quest-
ing gastronomic spirit. The main value of our present
experience was a certainty that no better cure for
drunkards existed than a wine-tour; or, if their tastes
had previously lain that way, a whisky-tour. As children, we had never believed that ridiculous story
about the girl behind the counter in the sweet-shop,
who was allowed, for the first two days, to gorge as
many sweets as she liked, and ever afterwards never
touched one; but now I accepted this legend, and knew
it to be solemn and unexaggerated truth.

Meanwhile we were leaving behind the Midi-
moins-un-quart, as the natives called their country
round Tain, for the true Midi did not begin till Montélimar, where the best nougat is manufactured. We
ascended roads described by Michelin as " *sinueuses
et pittoresques* " . . . until, without quite realizing
how it had happened, we discovered that chestnut-trees
had given way to Scotch firs, cypresses to poplars,
that there were no more vines or olives, no more
myrtle or juniper, no more peach, apricot, and cherry-

trees, with patches of Indian corn; but heather and whortleberries stretching as far as we could see; and crisp, bright autumn weather, the tinkle of cow-bells, sounding with that strange mountainy clearness, so different from cow-bells on the plains; and presently, to Johnny's rapture, a stretch of what he called *colchicum autumnale,* but kindly translated, for our amateur benefit, to a sweeter name, meadow saffron — great rosy crocus-cups. And then rowan-trees, brilliant waxen clusters of vermilion berries, lining the roads outside the villages; and behind every deep range of mountains, another, higher range, rising and dipping in glorious misty curves. "The road," said Michelin, staidly, " is sinuous and picturesque. . . ."

To say that we were surprised is a mild form of expression. Where were we? And what were these mountains? "Nobody tells me *anything!* " complained Humphrey, quoting, as he often did, the complaint of old James Forsyte, in *The Forsyte Saga.* Nobody had told any of us anything! We had all learnt geography. We knew that there were Alps and Pyrenees, and even the Cévennes and Juras; but nobody had told us that if we crossed France from east to west, from the Midi to Bordeaux, we should encounter a perfectly unknown range of mountains, that were neither Alps, Pyrenees, Cévennes, *nor* Juras. It gave us a lost, enchanted feeling. . . . We could find no clue in our guide-books, and no clue in our memories of what we had learnt at school.

And every instant the scenery grew grander, and the air colder, and white goats skipped from the road frantically up the bank to safety, as Flotsam rushed by. Under the pines were warm, floating smells of moss and whortleberries; the sun struck at the mountain ash and its clusters of glittering scarlet; the cows had that rich look of cream mixed with their paint; the passing oxen in the carts were banded with a kind of Egyptian head-dress, plaited with straw, across their brows; and whenever you listened attentively to the tinkle of cow-bells, you seemed to hear beyond them, higher and hidden, the rounder note of church-bells, and the splash of quickly running streams.

. . . Till at last, towards evening, we saw a slender aerial crag, and, at its very peak, a tiny Roman church, and behind it a wild sky, crimson, opal, and pale green; and our forlorn faerie sensations at the sight caused us to huddle down into our cloaks, and talk of homely things like beds and dinner, as we ran into the old town of Le Puy, and through a wide mediæval arch into the courtyard of the Grand Hôtel.

And, of course, in the Grand Hôtel the mystery of our day's glamourous journey into the hills was at once solved. The Syndicat d'Initiative had provided a stand in the hall, with booklets and leaflets and picture postcards, and every form of advertisement. We realized that we were in the regions of the Haute-Loire, or, alternatively, in the Velay; and that George Sand, a famous French novelist, had written about it thus: " This is not Switzerland as it is not so grand and awful. This is not Italy as it is finer! " And her deduction was correct both times. Apparently George Sand, on first arriving, had felt the same bewilderment as ourselves as to where she could possibly be. . . .

We learnt, furthermore, that the numerous streams " literally swarm with trouts, gudgeons, crayfish, and so on." Also that " owing to the purity of the air, the calm and rustic way of living prevailing everywhere, the villages and boroughs, all so attractive and quaint, and most of them provided with physicians, have charms of their own well calculated to entice visitors. Let us add that electric light is to be found in nearly every village, however so small." And, finally, that we were at a height of about three thousand nine hundred feet, and that " the felicitous peculiarities of its climate, combined with the diversified character of its landscapes and the natural resources to be met with in most of its localities, will always make it conspicuous among the other regions of the Massif Central of France."

— And after all that, we went down to dinner, with appetites stung by the sudden cold into a less fastidious and more appreciative state than they had been in during the past week. I believe we had soup, ham and eggs, and partridge; and drank a moderately good Richebourg 1915. The hotel was old-fashioned, and very well run; and we made a firm resolution, knowing that we had to start early next morning, that we would return one day to Le Puy, and stay at the Grand Hôtel, and explore. We even thought it possible that we might ascend the staircase of two hundred and eighty steps, spiralled into the rock, up to the tenth-century church of Saint Michel; but we did not definitely promise to do this, for there may have been strange gods among these mountains, who would hear us, and see to it that we did it; and two hundred and eighty spiral steps . . .

Le Puy enshrined the fascination of its surrounding mountains, without appalling me by any of the mountain awfulness that associates itself with the Dolomites or the higher Alps. It reminded me more of the Austrian Tyrol, without their backing of high peaks. It was exhilarating and hospitable, and you might rest there, and grow pure in soul and hungry in body, feeling that you were sojourning in a big farmyard. . . .

I was heartily sorry to leave it behind next morning, but I did not know then — we none of us knew — what was awaiting us for lunch at Saugues.

X
THE INN OF LEGEND

WE had no idea, as I have said, when we left
Tain-l'Hermitage, that the rather dull, straight,
white roads and poplars of my conventional imagination were to be exchanged for the enchantment of an
unknown mountain region. When we left Le Puy the
next morning, we saw by Michelin that it was a run of
forty-five kilometres to Saugues; there, at the Hôtel de
France, marked only with an egg-cup and spoon, we
might be able to get a tolerable lunch. We had no idea
that we were to be served with a lunch which is the
dream of all who sojourn haphazard through France.
There were no stars in Michelin to lure us to the Hôtel
de France; and nothing on the outside of the hotel itself — plain walls and a plain sign, an open courtyard
on to the village street, and an outside staircase to the
steep front-door.

THE INN OF LEGEND

We asked if we could eat. We were taken through the kitchen by another dark winding staircase into a small dining-room. At once, however, on entering it, we felt grateful, though it took a minute or two before we discovered why. . . . Ah yes, they had had the sense to keep their jalousies closed. The room was cool and dim in the green light filtering through; the blinding glare outside was blocked out, and there were no flies. Good! We asked the waiter, an efficient-looking man in white linen, what we could eat. " Trout and partridge," he replied, with humility. Well, yes, *faute de mieux*, trout and partridge. . . . We should have liked the worst-end-of-the-neck with some winter greens, but nevertheless — be it so! And the wine-list? Chablis, 1918, was our choice, and *vin ordinaire* to begin with.

The waiter quickly brought us some home-cured ham as an hors-d'œuvre. It was not very good. Only when the trout arrived, perfectly cooked, brown and delicious, with just the right accompaniment of butter and gravy, did we begin to suspect that our lunch might be above the egg-cup-and-spoon level.

After the trout, and without any waiting, *champignons* appeared, a big dish, crisp and brown and succulent, far too good for any remnants to be left upon our plates. Humphrey began to remind us gloomily that his surname was "Petit-Panche," and that he had very little room left for partridge! And then the waiter, who appeared to know by magic just when we were ready for each course, brought in, *not* the partridge, but what was probably the most tender rabbit in the world, cooked with tomato sauce; because he said that Madame feared we would not have enough with partridge alone! I have eaten the breast of chicken which has tasted like rabbit, but I have never yet eaten rabbit which tasted so like the breast of chicken.

When the partridges appeared, we reminded the waiter that he had murmured something about potatoes, and could we have them at the same time? He agreed, but was genuinely distressed at our wish. "You will see," he said, arriving with the potatoes, "that the flavours do not mingle well."

That man was an artist. He was quite right. The potato savoury, with its delicate crust of cheese, was spoilt by being eaten with the partridge. We left it till afterwards.

The next course was *écrevisses,* delicate little

MADAME AND HER STAFF AT SAUGUES

THE ENTRANCE TO THE CELLARS AT
CHÂTEAU LAFITE-ROTHSCHILD

river crayfish, cooked in brandy. I had given in by
now, and Humphrey was sobbing bitterly; but Johnny
plodded on; and Rosemary, in whom the gourmet had
for once triumphed over indigestion, came in a good
second.

The waiter cleared away the *écrevisses* rapidly
and silently, and produced — *flan*, he called it: a delicious pudding of white of egg and cream beaten up,
and sponge fingers to eat with it. Doubtless Madame
was afraid that we might still be hungry! After that,
we merely had to cope with cream-cheese, fruit, coffee,
and four *fines*.

The bill for the four of us, complete with wine,
mineral water, coffee, brandies, and service, amounted
to one hundred and eighteen francs, fifty centimes.
At the then rate of exchange, that is between fourteen
and fifteen shillings, roughly, in English money. With
the exception of the home-cured ham, not a single one
of the nine courses or so but was as delicately and in-
telligently cooked — created, one might say — as a
meal at any of the most famous five-star restaurants
of Paris or London.

When we went down, we spoke a few dazed
words of thanks and praise to Mme Anglade, the pro-

prietress, a thin, quiet wisp of a woman. "Ah, madame," she replied, " I was perhaps a good enough cook once, *mais on devient vieille, et on perd le courage!* "

"But one gets old, and one loses courage. . . ." We wondered, not unnaturally, with what sort of a dinner Madame would have served us *before* she lost courage?

She took a greal deal of coaxing before she would let us photograph her with her staff, including the efficient waiter, on the steps of the hotel. Certainly not a flamboyant woman!

XI
THAT——FRENCHMAN

AT Hermitage I had been smitten with what was afterwards diagnosed as a blow of the heat; so that I remember little of the scenery between Saugues and Aurillac, and still less from Aurillac to Bergerac, and on to Angoulême. We were still among mountains, but they sank to less jagged and more gracious outlines, and finally stretched in plateaux of purple heather and the ruddy brilliance of turning bracken.

At Aurillac, where I began to be feverish, and went to bed early, I can just recall my bright mauve bedroom, with mauve and orange curtains, before I sank off to sleep. Later on I was disturbed by vehement noises on the wooden floor of the room above me; thumpings and bangings, as though heavy wardrobes were being shifted. I complained of this to Johnny, when he joined me presently, and advanced the theory that the thumper and the banger, quiet for a moment, was a *commis voyageur*, who was leaving early next morning, and was packing his bulky cases in a fit of angry impatience at not having done better business at Aurillac. After a short silence the noise began again, if anything worse than before.

"Blast the fellow!" grumbled Johnny. He sprang on to the bed, and pounded a ferocious reprimand on the ceiling, with his hairbrush. Silence awhile. "*That's* taught him!" quoth Johnny, satisfied.

He was in bed and half asleep already when the *commis voyageur* — for I was now convinced of his calling — began to hurl his packing-cases afresh.

Johnny worked himself up into a terrific rage. It was eleven o'clock by now. Why couldn't the hotel . . . ? That —— (two syllables, accent on the first) of a Frenchman! . . . He pounded on the ceiling over and over again. That something of a Frenchman pounded back. International warfare seemed to have broken out, and I could not check it, nor, being angry myself, did I wish to check it. . . . I was so feverish, the room was so mauve, Johnny was so cross!

Another lengthy pause, in which we settled ourselves to sleep, hoping we had gained a moral victory. Then once more the banging and the thumping, and the loud rolling sounds of huge furniture being moved across the wooden floor. With blazing eyes and scarlet face Johnny delivered his final tattoo on the ceiling; and then, dressed only in pyjamas, rushed out of the room and upstairs.

Humphrey, too, had rushed out of his room, and was hastening downstairs as fast as his lameness would allow him.

"Look here, Johnny, there's a Something of a Frenchman gone quite mad in the room below us!"

And at the same moment: "There's a blasted commercial traveller gone quite mad in the room above us!" shouted Johnny.

———

XII
CYRANO'S TOWN AND THE HOS-
TELRY OF THE THREE PILLARS

BEFORE we came to Bergerac, we passed beneath the high walls of Saint-Flour, a fortified
town on a hill, crested by two towers. These little
huddled towns, safe within their battlements, are as
magical as islands, because one can walk all round
them, making a spell of the circle. Humphrey, who is
quite crazy on fortified towns, and spends hours over
his maps and Michelin Guide, working out where he
can possibly bend and divert our tour to include as
many of these as possible, drove slower and slower as
we approached Saint-Flour. It was against the rules,
those perpetual rules that we are always making for
our own discomfort, to stop for the night before sunset, unless some accident to the car, or lack of accom-
modation further on, forced us to it. Humphrey longed

to stay the night at Saint-Flour. We all were fascinated, only perhaps not quite so hopelessly enamoured; but it was only a quarter to five. " Shall we? . . ." I asked tentatively. Humphrey set his jaw. Flotsam suddenly leapt ahead, at a speed of seventy kilometres an hour. Saint-Flour was passed, dwindled, vanished. Perhaps we should never see it again.

At Beaulieu-sur-Dordogne, where we lunched moderately well, the natives took us for the " Australian Circus," which had been advertised as shortly due to appear. I do not know why. I only know that when we went to Budapest the year before, and our luggage was examined at the customs, they asked us if we were cabaret performers — and then I did not know why, either.

On the wall of the room where we lunched was a map clock-face on cardboard, with certain hours shaded, and other hours brightened, and such admonitions as " *Parlez bas,*" " *Marchez doucement,*" " *Pensez aux autres,*" appropriately marked across the hours towards sleeping-time. Johnny and I significantly drew Humphrey's attention to " *Marchez doucement* " and " *Pensez aux autres,*" but to no effect;

Humphrey still thought it had all been our fault at Aurillac.

We slept the night at Bergerac, after a run beside the Dordogne, which is a good river, gracious and companionable, as indeed most rivers are. The hotel we went to was dark and rather stuffy, and our waiter at dinner had obviously once been a music-hall comedian, for he never stopped joking, and when I asked for an omelet, said: " I will bring you one, madame, made with eggs! " . . . That kind of joke!

Michelin had informed us that the speciality of Bergerac was simply " *vin*," which seemed to be of interest to us. The walls of Bergerac had everywhere been plastered with advertisements proclaiming that " *Bergerac, Ses Vins* " must not be missed; and on the *carte des vins*, Bordeaux and Burgundy and Rhone wines were squeezed away into an insignificant corner, while Mombazillac, the wine for which Bergerac was famous, occupied two and a half pages.

We began to be excited about Mombazillac. It was a fine swaggering name, to begin with, a name like an oath of Gascony — for certainly we were in Gascony now, if we used the old names of the provinces: " *Ce sont les cadets de Gascogne.*" So we told the wine-waiter to bring the very best Mombazillac on his list. I think he chose a 1918. It was poured out, a rich gold. We tasted it. . . .

Mon Dieu!

It is an understatement that this wine was sweet. Sugar is sweet, and syrup, and figs, and honey. But Mombazillac was sweeter than all these. We put it down hastily, and looked about for the cruet-stand. The wine-waiter, not the joking one, but a man who took Mombazillac seriously, hovered about us, ready to refill our glasses, ready to hear our words of appreciation. The hotel seemed to us a little too gloomy and sinister, and we did not care, unarmed as we were, without even a revolver to use inside the car, to express our real opinion of Mombazillac. We each finished our glasses, and Johnny heroically finished the bottle. The waiter suggested another bottle, but they said that Madame — meaning me — was " *très souffrante* " (a phrase which we found very useful in France, varying the victim as we went) and quickly left the dining-room.

A little later, Humphrey advanced the theory, which struck me as a good one, that white Mombazillac was responsible for Cyrano's sloppy behaviour over

Roxane and Christian and the letters. " That sort of sacrifice which does nobody any good is just sheer silliness," he argued, fretfully, still tasting the wine on his palate, " and I could never make it out, as Cyrano was a clever man; but of course if he had been drinking Mombazillac in any quantity . . ."

I woke early the next morning. Johnny was standing silhouetted at the window. The sun had just risen. We were high on the third floor, and a panorama of steep roofs, a cluster of ruddy browns and sepias and greys, was spread below our window.

" I suppose," he said, slowly, staring down, " that to thousands of people this would seem terribly romantic — to wake up in the morning and look out at the roofs of Bergerac."

And suddenly, to me as well as to Johnny and to those thousands of people, it did seem incredibly romantic. *Cyrano de Bergerac* was one of my favourite plays. I love rant passionately, when it is well done — a weakness in me which began, probably, at the age of nine, when I read *Under Two Flags* for the first time. I love Ouida, I love Rostand, I love Ruritania, I loved Lewis Waller. There is too little rant in our daily lives.

. . . Et samedi, vingt-six, une heure avant dîné,
Monsieur de Bergerac est mort assassiné.

At Bergerac I bought a hat for one and three-
pence. One of those wide fringed sun-hats, in green
and orange, that the peasants wore thereabouts. Once
I bought a hat off a barrow in the Verona market, and
that was cheaper; and once I bought a hat in Paris
from Jeanne Lanvin, and that was not so cheap.

(And all the time I was growing more and
more feverish.)

On September the nineteenth we passed
through three villages, called Maison Jeannette, Les
Trois Frères, and Rossignol; but before my imagination had grouped them into the fairy-tale their inno-
cence and simplicity deserved, we arrived at Périgueux, where we lunched at the Hôtel de France —
spécialité: pâté de foie gras, and very excellent it was.
Here we met another wine-waiter surnamed Swingbottle, who succeeded in ruining what might have
been a tolerable 1914 Château Lafite; and grimly
Johnny retold the old story of the connoisseur who
said apprehensively to his new butler: " Jenkins, have
you shaken the wine? " " No, sir, but I *will!* "

When we arrived at Angoulême, towards evening, I went firmly to bed, and sent for the doctor. Luckily, the Nouvel Hôtel des Trois Piliers, a two-house hotel, with a star for its cooking, was one of those which we placed easily among the first half-dozen on our tour; it should have had stars for kindness, for comfort, cleanliness, and charm, as well as for its cuisine.

The room in which I was to spend the next two days was white and blue, and restful. It had hot and cold water laid on, a balcony outside, and a bath-room adjoining. Below the balcony was the cheerful little town of Angoulême, and the cheerful little fair, which I have mentioned before, and which I recognized again with horror. There seemed no doubt but that the merry-go-rounds and the gaiety would be bound to go on — and the friendly, pleasant-faced chambermaid agreed with me — till midnight; because it was Sunday; and the people liked to divert themselves. This was not exactly what an invalid with a temperature, aching limbs, and a strong desire for sleep would have chosen to divert her; and the weather was too hot again for closed windows, now that we had come down from the mountains.

However, strangely enough, this bogy vanished. A fair is such a welded mass of noise, such an incessant roaring waterfall of sound, that it does not disturb as isolated noises might do. The trampling and the voices and the music blend into a colossal symphony. Your senses are at first stunned; then, curiously enough, you are soothed by it. The noise is mighty enough to uphold your thoughts or your dreams, to bear them along in a torrent. . . .

I was rather glad of the fair that went on beneath my window at Angoulême, although I could not yet see it.

Rosemary and I had agreed beforehand that the doctor, when he materialized, must be either of the kind that has a square black beard, speaks in a funereal voice, and carries a little shiny black dispatch-case; or else the round and rosy kind, with a bald head and a jaunty little moustache. When the latter appeared, complete in every detail, at the bedroom door, it was difficult not to giggle. He told me all about the blow of the heat which I had sustained, aggravated by wine and neglect; and prescribed two days in bed, many medicines, and, above all things important, a diet of water to drink, and mashed potatoes, tapioca, and vermicelli to eat. When I see tapioca, not only my gorge, but my complex rises, and I revert instantly to my childish remedy of throwing it on the floor. Latterly, since I have lived in Italy, I have done the same to vermicelli.

That left the mashed potatoes. . . .

"You came here by car?" said the doctor. "What is your car? A Fiat? Three of mine are Renaults, and the other a Citroën!" — And on this, having made his impression, he went.

I do not know what Rosemary and Johnny and Humphrey ate during the next two days, as, with merciful tact, they kept it from me. I could see, however, from their faces that they were pleased and happy. Meanwhile I ate mashed potatoes, read Trollope for the first time, and listened to the fair.

Trollope is the most delightful of authors to be reading for the first time, on a wine-tour through France. He is so absorbingly English. The murmur of Barchester politics and Barchester lovers, the gossip of Barchester parsons and deans and bishops, ran like a sleepy stream under the constant jostle of new pictures that were queer and foreign and brightly coloured. I was immeasurably grateful to Trollope. His books were so comfortingly long. You could

nibble and nibble away at them, and be satisfied that
there would still be more to nibble on the morrow:
*Doctor Thorne, Framley Parsonage, The Small House
at Allington,* and *The Last Chronicle of Barset,* carried in small editions, lasted me from Avignon to Bordeaux, from Bordeaux to Beaune, from Beaune to
Avignon again. I felt myself being simultaneously en-
riched by wine, by travel, and by Trollope. Why had
I never been forced into reading him before? But I
am glad I was not. By happy delusions about dullness
and stodginess, and by a miracle of good luck, I now
had Trollope when and where I most needed him.

On our third day at Angoulême I was able to
get up and go downstairs for a little, very light dinner; and now my companions thought fit to inform me
that the cooking was excellent, that they were on terms
of the greatest friendliness with the proprietor, with
Madame, and with the whole staff, including several
puppies, and a most sympathetic and understanding
head waiter; and that this hotel at Angoulême was to
get full marks. I was able to corroborate this, especially the part about the head waiter, who was most
fatherly, and humorous without losing dignity, and an
artist at his job. The very way in which he poured out

the wonderful 1873 Cognac into the right size and shape of glass, well warmed " *pour déguster*," proved this at once.

The only blot on our pleasure in the meal was a horrid crying child, peevish and voluble, at another table. It could not have been more than three or four years old, and at ten o'clock it was still sitting there, a nuisance adored by its relatives. This was not the first time that we had noticed the inability of French parents to put their children to bed at a proper time. . . . " There was a lot to be said for King Herod," remarked Humphrey at last; and " Herod's Bane " was our future name for each of that species, whenever encountered. Some parents did not appear to like this name. Rosemary remarked to quite a broad-minded pair in other respects: " *Your* Herod's Bane is really very sweet! " And they did not seem pleased.

We drank, or rather the others drank, a Chambertin, 1919, with their dinner, although we were so near Bordeaux. I gather they had had, the night before, an excellent Mission Haut Brion, 1919, but that to-night the Burgundians were to be considered. And this led the conversation to yet another battle in the

war between the Bordelais and the Burgundians; a
war that never flagged, not at Burgundy nor yet at
Bordeaux. The wine-tour which was supposed to decide our war most finally, left it in the exact stage that
it had been in to begin with. . . .

XIII

OF THE WAR BETWEEN THE BOR-
DELAIS AND THE BURGUNDIANS

THIS had been the outbreak of war:

In 1924 Johnny and I had dined at the Hôtel de Paris in Monte Carlo. The *sommelier* was a lean, distinguished gentleman, with a silvery moustache of the type that inspires confidence, and eyes wrinkled with ironic amusement, possibly at some of the palates he had encountered. He had recommended Château Margaux, 1899, as being the best wine in his cellars. We had drunk very little good wine at the time, and that special Château Margaux was a revelation. I had not dreamt that there existed a wine with a bouquet to provoke such longings, nor a velvet to inspire such dreams, nor an after-taste to lull longings and dreams with such content. So that it naturally followed that thereafter, whenever wine was mentioned, Johnny and

I would look at each other with the secret glance of those who have been privileged above all other mortals . . . and then, reverently, we told about Château Margaux, 1899; reverently, but not eloquently, for, as I have so frequently said, the grander the wine, the more elusively it slides away from the descriptive phrase. But upon the rock of this superb '99 we built our faith in claret.

When Humphrey and Rosemary came along, and between us we had exhausted the topic of mysterious Hermitage, they, to our amazement, began to babble, as fools will babble, of Burgundy, which they had the temerity to place above Bordeaux in their estimation; not side by side, as king to queen — this we might have suffered —but definitely, in relation to Bordeaux, as emperor to a middle-class but well-meaning mayor. Johnny and I did not argue. We merely promised them a dinner at the Hôtel de Paris in Monte Carlo.

And after a lapse of time, there we all four met to dine. I trust that our manner as hosts did not convey too blatantly the thought: " You poor dunces! This is to be your hour of initiation! " but it probably did. We were quite intoxicated, you see, with anticipation. The same *sommelier* took our casual order for a bottle of '99 Château Margaux. He seemed pleased that we had remembered it.

" But it must all be drunk this year," he said.

The wine was poured out. We twiddled the stems of the glasses, and then slowly raised it and smelt. . . . Yes, there it was again, that divine bouquet! Our unspoken panic lest time might have exaggerated our sense of values now vanished. It was all right, quite all right, the same bouquet. . . . And on Humphrey's face and Rosemary's I was pleased to notice the dawn of an immense, though reluctant, respect.

Then we sipped.

I may as well be swift and brutal — to myself, for it is not likely that even the most sympathetic will care as much as I cared, and Johnny.

The taste was quite different from the year before.

Something had happened.

If it had only been worse, if it had been definitely corked, we could, of course, have told the *sommelier,* who would have apologized profusely, and brought us another bottle. But it was not corked. It was just not such a good bottle — perhaps already a year past its delicate perfection; a nice claret, but not supreme. That surpassing fragrance had lied.

. . . "Yes, it *is* good!" said Humphrey and Rosemary, politely.

"Isn't it?" Johnny and I agreed. We had not yet compared impressions, nor even glanced at each other, so we could not be sure. . . . Perhaps it had been like this last year, and we had forgotten. Later on, when we were alone, I questioned Johnny anxiously; and he, at the same moment, began to question me with equal anxiety.

But it was bad luck that at that dinner of all dinners, arranged for the conversion of two stiff-necked rebels — stiff-tongued, I should say — Château Margaux '99 should have failed us.

They were very nice about it. They could afford to be. Naturally they did not believe in the miracle and the rapture of our first experience. Why should they? And when again they started talking of Burgundy, we had no answer ready. We answered brokenly, for our pride was in tatters. . . .

This is an almost unbearably sad story.

Then Humphrey and Rosemary left Italy and

went back to England, motoring through France. Apparently they spent a night at Mâcon. We had a postcard from Rosemary, scribbled with hilarious impudence above a view of the River Saône: " Had a most marvellous bottle of old Romanée-Conti. Humphrey and I drank a toast: Burgundy for ever! Death to Bordeaux! "

Then came the wine-tour.

You will perceive that there must necessarily have been an atmosphere of high tension, when the Burgundians and the Bordelais went forth as one party to Bordeaux and Burgundy. The Côte du Rhône was mutual ground. We all approved of the wine; we were all pleasantly surprised by it. In Hermitage the opposing forces could rest and lay down their arms and utter pæans of praise; but the great question itself could be decided only in Bordeaux and in Burgundy. These were the battle-fields. Here luck must take sides again. Here or there, one side or the other must lay down its arms and declare the other's victory. We had all pledged our stubborn souls that we would be honest, and that if we met a wine without peer in the opposing kingdom, we would acknowledge it.

Now here we were at Angoulême, on the outskirts of Bordeaux. Surely we could not fail to find at least one great claret of a great year within the next few days? Yet so far we had been disappointed in the clarets we had sampled. That was the trouble with claret. When Humphrey brought forward this point, over our glasses of '73 Cognac, at the Hôtel des Trois Piliers, remarking that with a claret, whatever the label and whatever the year, you were disappointed nine times out of ten, we could not but own that he was right.

"And with Burgundy," he went on, "nine times out of ten you are not disappointed. Nine times out of ten you get an excellent wine."

And again I owned that he was right: "But my point is — " and in my mind's eye wavered a row of ten bottles, the vision dividing itself into groups of nine and one, one and nine, and then forming again, dark soldiers with white labels — " my point is that the Tenth Bottle of Bordeaux compensates for the other nine, and counts more — quite alone it counts more — than the nine excellent bottles of Burgundy that haven't disappointed you."

— What I wanted to say, but I was not quite

rude enough yet, though I was going to be in a few minutes, was that only a humdrum palate, which at all times preferred safety to a glorious risk, could prefer Burgundy merely for the uninspired reason that the *average* Burgundy was very much better than the *average* Bordeaux. All this I was to stammer angrily and incoherently when Rosemary had further goaded me by comparing every claret she had yet tasted to red ink.

" It's so acid! " she complained. " It pulls my mouth together, and afterwards my tongue feels like blotting-paper." Her metaphors were all drawn from a stationer's shop.

Johnny retorted, flinging himself into the middle of one of Humphrey's measured statements, by a full-blooded attack on Burgundy: " The whole trouble about Burgundy is, to my mind, that it's just a straightforward, sound wine. It has all the excellent qualities of any really worthy or excellent person; but there's no excitement about it. It's not provocative. It doesn't remind you of anything except itself. It has a good Burgundy bouquet, and a good Burgundy body, and a good Burgundy after-taste. It keeps well, and is very rarely disappointing, and that's that. But

Bordeaux — oh, you risk your luck again and again! It's capricious — granted; it's delicate; it's always letting you down " — we thought of the Château Margaux — " but *when* —— Oh, that once, that Tenth Bottle is worth it! It's elusive and glorious. It simply gets you, so that no other wine can ever mean the same again; and if the bad clarets are fifty times worse and fifty times oftener bad than the bad Burgundies —— "

"They are," interrupted Rosemary. " They give me indigestion."

" — the good one, when it comes along, transcends every first-class old Burgundy that has ever yet been put on the table."

"Wait till you taste that Romanée-Conti! " cried Rosemary.

"Well, but no Burgundy I've ever tasted —— "

" No, that's just it. When you do . . . But we, on the other hand, have tasted what's supposed to be the most wonderful claret of all."

" Oh, that Château Margaux —— That was simply our rotten luck. But you never tasted the Château Margaux which we had the year before."

"Can't expect us to believe in a wine we haven't tasted."

"You can't expect *us* to. I've had Chambertin — Corton —— "

"I'm not worrying at all," said Rosemary, with a large, radiating placidity, "because I know, I'm absolutely confident, that the minute you get to Mâcon and you taste that Romanée-Conti, you'll say: 'This is the most wonderful wine there is, and no other wine can touch it!'"

Johnny and I smiled. "Of course we'll say so if we think it," we said courteously. What did we care? — before we came to Burgundy; and close at hand, now, were the vineyards of Médoc: Château Latour, Château Lafite, Mouton Rothschild. . . . Even if these people remained callous and unreceptive to the subtle enchantments of Bordeaux's Tenth Bottle, the loss was theirs. It was for such as they that Burgundy was invented. . . .

"My point is," said Humphrey, and I believe, from the menacing glow in his eyes, that he had been saying: "My point is — " for quite a long time before any of us would attend; "My point is, that even when you get a real super-claret, which only happens about twice in a lifetime, and so isn't worth all the bad clarets you've had to drink meanwhile —— "

I interrupted him, of course. It is Humphrey's fate to be interrupted, because the streak of formality in his character compels him always to set forth his arguments in a logical and orderly way; whereas we rush them out and scatter them, confusedly, perhaps, and stammering, but still they are got out: " And *my* point is, that to us it *is* worth while. It may not be to you, but it is to us. We're idealists. ' We needs must love the highest,' etc. ' Ay, but a man's reach should exceed his grasp, or what's a claret for? ' — Even if it weren't one in ten, even if it were one in a hundred —— "

" My point is," Humphrey continued, restraining his exasperation with difficulty, " that your pleasure in claret doesn't last beyond the first glass, not even in the best claret. The second and third glasses lose their charm; lose their taste, even; whereas the pleasure in Burgundy is accumulative up to the third or fourth glass."

" My point is — " said Johnny.

— And: " My point is — " from Rosemary.

We continued to argue for an hour or two yet, and parted that night in a mutual atmosphere of biding our time. . . .

On the morrow we set out for Bordeaux.

XIV

CHAPON FIN AND CHAPEAU ROUGE

A S we drove along between the crowding traffic of the quays at Bordeaux, we sank a little timidly into our seats, with the sensation that a fortnight spent in little friendly villages, and speeding along kindly roads, had robbed us of our city confidence. Bordeaux appeared overwhelming, and even the protection of Michelin seemed to be withdrawn from us, and only his cold, curt directions remained. Altogether we spent only three days in Bordeaux and were glad to escape from it; a pitiful confession for four swaggering cosmopolitans, hitherto at home in London, Paris, Rome, Vienna, and Budapest, with a touch of patronage for those dwelling gently in rural pastures and unfrequented mountains.

In Bordeaux was the famous restaurant of the Chapon Fin, marked with four stars. The Chapeau

Rouge, slightly less celebrated, had also four stars; and the Restaurant de la Presse had three. There are two other three-star restaurants in Bordeaux; and by way of a commentary on the excellence of all these, most of the hotels were marked in brackets " *meublés* "; that is to say, one could only sleep and not eat. *Bien!* In Bordeaux we did as the Bordelais. After our first night's surprise at discovering that ours was the only table occupied in the hotel restaurant, we lunched and dined out.

I am still mourning the wanton destruction of a bottle of 1914 Château Cos d'Estournel which we drank that night; it was our first experience of how little the wine-waiters in that region appreciated the extreme delicacy of the treasures of which they are guardian. I know that a wine which behaves all the time like an invalid wife: " You mustn't shake me! You're tilting me an inch too much! My dear, *do* take care of my sediment. . . . Just a wee bit too warm! Just a shade too cold! " does exact the utmost vigilance; but nevertheless I can hardly bear to think of the glorious bouquet of the Cos d'Estournel, that familiar claret bouquet, which to me is like none other in the world . . . and then to

remember its brilliance clouded thickly with sediment.

Especially as Humphrey said he did not care
for it, with an inflexion of " I told you so! "

However, my spirits recovered in the night,
and it was in a state of high expectation that we went
to lunch at the Chapon Fin the next day. We were surprised, certainly, when " The Good Capon," which
from its name we had pictured as small and intimate,
proved to be in reality a vast apartment, decorated as
a grotto. With no wish to criticize, I wondered merely
why a grotto. Had the man who originally conceived
the idea read T. E. Browne? Did he think it " a love-
some place, God wot; fringed plot, fern grot . . ." ?
It was exactly like a restaurant in fancy dress — Enter
the Chapon Fin, dressed as a grotto!

Neither was the atmosphere intimate. The
wine-waiter and the *maître d'hôtel* were just the merest
shade aloof and preoccupied with their European
reputation. I did not feel cherished at the Chapon Fin,
but the cooking was undoubtedly divine. We ordered
de la maison whenever possible, feeling that here it
would be worth while to follow the chef's own inspirations.

Hors-d'œuvres — a marvellous selection. Sole *de la maison* — steamed, with mussels darkening the sauce. *Pintade,* again in a most glorious sauce, enshrining mushrooms and other happy items; and then *fraises de la maison,* delicious little wood-strawberries, snuggling beneath a smooth eider-down of cream, faintly flavoured with almond.

We left the selection of our wines to the *sommelier,* and again I was slightly disappointed, though I believe he acted for the best. Perhaps he deemed it a pity to bring out his solemn great wines for what must have seemed to him like a light luncheon, lightly undertaken.

" You are eating guinea-fowl," he said. " With guinea-fowl you must have a Petrus."

Probably he was right. It was not for us to say; so we had a Château Petrus, 1913, Pomerol, first growth; preceded, however, by a Chevalier, which is a delightful white wine to drink with fish. The mating of Petrus with *pintade* may have been predestined by all the connoisseurs, but it just did not appeal to me; the Petrus was too like Burgundy, and not enough like Bordeaux!

Humphrey and Rosemary liked it.

The *fine* Champagne of 1869 could not have been bettered.

We dined at the Restaurant de la Presse, a much homelier place, where we were waited upon by women, who all had the air of being daughters of the house. Oddly enough this was the first restaurant in France where we were given fish-knives and forks. The meal was mostly memorable for a most beautiful Chablis 1899; a rather puzzling Chablis; for whereas from its fragrance and flavour it seemed undoubtedly genuine, its colour was a very deep gold; the true Chablis, so I had been warned over and over again, is always very pale and faintly greenish in hue.

The Chablis was followed by a Marquis de Terme 1911, a fourth growth of claret; I had sampled it a year before, from the cellars of Messrs. Steiner of San Remo; a fine and silky vintage of 1900. From the same cellar came a superlatively good Mouton Rothschild 1917; one of my sterner friends had told me that I was committing infanticide by daring to drink a 1917 Mouton Rothschild; and I suppose he was right, and that I ought to have waited another fifteen or twenty years, nursing my desire; nevertheless, those two clarets, the Marquis de Terme, and the eight-year-old Mouton Rothschild, were for some inexplicable reason better than every wine, except one, that I was to drink in Bordeaux itself, with the great Médoc country not five miles away, and Haut-Brion just beyond the city gates.

— "Not very good, dear," said Rosemary, as she sipped the 1911 Marquis de Terme; and Humphrey said nothing at all.

I tried to console myself with quail, wrapped picturesquely in a strip of bacon-fat and a vine-leaf. I said that that dinner was memorable for the fish-knives and forks, and for the Chablis. I have forgotten one other outstanding incident, the collapse of Johnny, his one collapse during the whole tour, from too much food and drink. By an irony of chance, he had the day before invented and added to our perpetual vocabulary the word "glotto," signifying "gloriously glutted and blotto." It seemed to us a good word; we hailed it with applause. . . . And now none of us dared use it, even in a whisper!

On our last night in Bordeaux we went to dine at the Chapeau Rouge. It was the most successful of our dinners. From the moment we entered, we had a

premonition that here all would be well. We liked the
plain room, with its Wedgwood panels. We liked the
aura of the *maître d'hôtel,* and decided at once that
we preferred to be waited on by men rather than by
women; " There's always a touch of ' Come on, Father,
dinner's ready! ' about waitresses," remarked Humphrey.

The *maître d'hôtel* gave us his full and interested attention. He was a merry man, but not too
merry. You must not be too merry where food and
drink are in question — genial, but not jovial, should
be the waiter's motto. He only made one mistake,
in suffering three of us to order cold sole in aspic.
It was an oppressively hot evening, and our first impulse was to order almost everything iced; but he
should have warned us, with a touch of severity, that
sole is a fish that loses its flavour when cold. True, it
was served with such a wonderful mayonnaise that
this in itself was compensation; but Rosemary had decided independently on *cêpes bordelais;* and they
smelt and looked so rich and delicious, and her expression on tasting them was so ecstatic, that Humphrey and Johnny and I could not refrain from beg-
ging for alms from her plate, just enough to taste, for

she declared that never before had she eaten them so beautifully cooked.

This is the recipe for *cêpes bordelais,* as spoken by the head waiter of the Chapeau Rouge, who had received it from the lips of the chef of the Chapeau Rouge, in the manner that legends are passed on, reverently — and often inaccurately, for I cannot vouch that this is right: the heads of the *cêpes* are put into a casserole, with olive-oil, and cooked very slowly. In a separate pan have been cooking the stalks, chopped up. Take the stalks out of the pan and cover them with chopped parsley and garlic; and in a third pan bring some more oil to the boil. Put the stalks, etc., into this pan, pour the whole mixture over the heads, and serve.

Unfortunately, the *maître d'hôtel* turned round just at the moment when the three little dabs of *cêpes bordelais* were being shovelled on to the plates that had lately contained sole and mayonnaise. And, poor man, he nearly died of shock! Rushing forward, but too late, he declared, sobbing, that he would have brought clean plates, clean cutlery, more *cêpes, anything* . . . rather than that a royal dish should meet with such indignity! He was, of course, quite right.

We apologized humbly, and did our best to recover a
little esteem in his eyes. I think he recognized a glim-
mer of intelligence in our discussion over the wine-
list; for he did not begin, in the way of most *som-
meliers* when we asked them which was the gem of
their cellars; for they usually took such a question as
a confession of our own incompetence, and began to
inform us indulgently that Bordeaux was a different
wine from Burgundy, and that the quality of wine
varied according to the date on the label. . . .

(*" Tiens? "* said Rosemary.)

Humphrey and Rosemary, when they had last
travelled through France, had made one other discovery besides the great Romanée-Conti at Mâcon.
They had drunk Pouilly-sur-Loire in its native home,
and recalled it as a delicious light white wine, very
individual and fresh, with a flavour of flowers that is
usually the property of Rhine wine alone. We drank
Pouilly-sur-Loire now, and agreed with them in their
liking for it, although they assured us it was not quite
so good as doubtless we should have later, on our
way to Beaune.

The big wine on which we banked our hopes
was Château Ausone, that great first growth of Saint-

Émilion. The date was 1906. The bottle was treated, we were profoundly thankful to see, in the manner of a cradled heir to a great house, where no more can be expected.

After all our disappointments the first second of savouring and tasting was one of almost unbearable tension. . . .

Then Johnny and I sighed in relief.

It was all right.

It was more than all right.

There were many *beaux gestes* on the part of Humphrey and Rosemary, which we as graciously received. Château Ausone had all the best characteristics which had won Bordeaux her crown and queenship. It was suave and melodious, with a marvellous bouquet. It lay softly on the tongue; and when it had slipped down the throat, it left behind it an echo and a dream.

There is always something hopelessly comic about duck; and I am afraid that when I begin raving about the duck which had been selected by me, and by me alone, at the Chapeau Rouge, I shall be rudely accused of anticlimax. But, you know, that duck! —

you could almost drink it! Without any action of the jaw it simply melted away in your mouth.

It was the tenderest duck I have ever eaten;
And they served it with *petits pois*,
And bacon,
And tiny frail onions.

XV
MAINLY ABOUT MÉDOC

DIRECTLY we had presented our introductions to M. Louis Calvet, one of the biggest wine-merchants in Bordeaux, we saw that our responsibilities were all over. We might trustfully submit, or we might rebel, but in any case the result would be the same. For M. Calvet was a man of destiny. Large, jovial, kindly, helpful, he was of the type whose will and boundless vitality voluminously embraced all lesser wills, as a hurricane scatters temporary breezes and renders them of no account. The whole is greater than the part; our little futile baby plans were the part; M. Calvet's One Plan quickly and competently settled the next four days for us; gave orders, cards of introduction; rang up his ambassadors and minions in various outlying parts of the Bordeaux region of vine-yards; wrote down times, names, and addresses; asked us a few genial questions; blew us through his immense cellars, and out again; patted us on the heads and told us to be good children, and learn all about wine, and if there was anything he could do, ever, to assist us, we had only to call on him. . . .

We tried, in return for all this collossal organization on our behalf, to falter out a proposal that if there were anything we could do for M. Calvet . . . ? But the words died on our lips. It was so obviously absurd that we, little pygmies, should imagine that we could aid so powerful a giant. M. Calvet himself seemed to think so. He smiled and thanked us, and shook us warmly by the hand — merciful heavens, his grip! He was just off to Africa or to Beaune, I forget which — perhaps he had just come from Africa and was going to Beaune. A little airy *badinage* — I think that is the *mot juste* — fluttered between us about old wine and young ladies and *beauté du diable*. And I made an epigram in which was enshrined a pretty compliment to his wines, and he was mightily pleased. Everything about M. Calvet was mighty. One could never imagine him unsuccessful or shrinking. I have the utmost respect and admiration for him, but if I saw very much of him, I should develop an inferiority complex.

sleeve and said out loud, as we neared the door: " Yes, but isn't he going to *give* us a bottle, now? Aren't *we* to drink any of it? " Apparently this was not part of the ceremonial. I decided, not without cause, that the Rothschilds had too much good wine, and I too little.

The next-door estate was Mouton-Rothschild, and Saint-Julien was not far off; but we did not stop at either of these, nor at Château Latour, but went on to Château Margaux, which, we were told, contained the largest wine-vault in existence. The château, from outside, was exactly one's idea of a *sous-préfecture;* but the great pillared hall into which we were shown was unforgettable. Rows and rows of casks lay parallel on the floor, stretching away on either side towards a Gothic vanishing point in the far distance. They each had a little glass stopper, which glimmered faintly through the religious gloom. Everything at Château Margaux was of Brobdingnagian proportions. The huge oak vats were the largest vats I saw in France, and equally immense were the roomy presses. Here, in ten days or a fortnight, men would be trampling out the grapes with their feet. The vineyards were like wide flat moors; they rolled back and back to the horizon. I was glad that Château Margaux, which

THE GREAT VATS AT CHÂTEAU MARGAUX

WINE-CARTS AT CHÂTEAU MARGAUX

I shall always feel is more my wine than any other, had this triumphant aspect.

We were given, by a different version of the perpetual Simon the Cellarer, some Château Margaux to taste from the wood: 1925, and then 1924. '25 was light, and would surprisingly soon be fit to drink, much before '24, which was, however, a more promising vintage. I vowed a silent oath that in 1945 I would send for a bottle of Château Margaux 1924, and discover whether this prognostication was right.

But meanwhile here we were in the land of promise itself, in the kingdom of Médoc, and had not yet broached one memorable bottle. There was no choice of places to lunch; Pauillac was the only little village with a restaurant in the heart of the Médoc country. We lunched out of doors. The weather was hot and sunny; and the prospect, facing a wide estuary of the Gironde, could not have been bettered. But it was the worst lunch of the whole tour: bad food, served in a slovenly fashion, and with interminable intervals; and a bottle of Bordeaux wine which was so inferior and sour that I cannot even remember its name, and do not want to. It was too cruel a disappointment that here, where of all places one should have been given sumptuous food and heroic wine, there should be no alternative to this mediocre meal. Where was the usually vivid imagination of the French, not to foresee the effect of such an anticlimax on strangers visiting the most renowned of the Bordeaux vineyards, Château Lafite, Château Latour, and Château Margaux?

"This is very bad wine," said Rosemary, at lunch, " terribly like red ink! "

And Humphrey nodded, and said not a word.

XVI
"BUT THEN, HOW IT WAS SWEET!"

STILL firmly entangled in the web of M. Calvet's benevolent efficiency, we drove on the morning of September 23rd to the Hôtel de Lion d'Or, at Langon, in the Sauternes district. He had given us a card with, quite simply, the name of an unknown man on it, the name of the hotel, and the time of day that we were to arrive there. Trustfully we delivered this card, not quite knowing what was to happen to us. They seemed a little fogged, too, at the hotel, but they showed us into a private room, with the table all ready for three. Then they left us alone.

We waited — it seemed for hours — growing hungrier every minute. We could not order the lunch, for we did not know whether M. Calvet had ordered it for us — we dared not run counter to the arrangements of M. Calvet, you see! — or whether we were the guests of the unknown name on the card. On the other hand, the hotel might be waiting for us to order our own lunch, and do it quickly, so as not to keep the unknown name waiting, when it arrived to take us round the châteaux. Finally, it occurred to us that neither the room nor the table nor the knives and forks might be meant for us at all.

At last, desperately, I went into the kitchen and made further inquiries. A very good-looking waiting-maid, tall and strong like Diana, suddenly pushed her way forward, laughing, and affirming that she knew all about it. It was she who had taken the message; and yes, please, we were to lunch at once. We would be called for at one-thirty. Much relieved, I returned to the dining-room, but we still did not know if we were to be allowed to order our own lunch. Apparently not, for she arrived with the hors-d'œuvres and a menu already written. Doubtfully she inquired whether " our chauffeur " would eat with us or not? We looked at Humphrey. He seemed fairly neat and clean, and we decided that we might show thus much condescension, and put up with him for once, making it clear that we were not thereby creating a precedent. . . . So the girl laid another place at the table.

Presently she brought in two bottles of wine. We had reached that stage of sophistication where we were really not quite happy when faced with the wine of another's choice. " Did M. Calvet — ? " I asked, doubtfully. No, not M. Calvet; the unknown gentleman, whose name was on the card, he had chosen our wines for us. She poured out the Cheval Blanc, a Graves Saint-Émilion of 1923, and then left us to it.

It was hopelessly sweet, of course, sweeter even than our apprehensions. The awful feeling of helplessness increased. *Where* was our host? *Who* was our host? Sweet wine, and nobody to kick for it! We left most of it, and hoped for relief from the next bottle. The food itself was good.

With the *poulet en cocotte* the second bottle was opened for us — Sauterne Sigalas-Rabaud, 1922.

Perhaps the best way of describing it would be to state that by force of its sweeter sweetness, it made the first wine seem quite dry; in fact, that was its principal merit, that whenever we took a sip of the Sigalas-Rabaud, and then, quickly on top of it, the Cheval Blanc, we could find real enjoyment in the Cheval Blanc.

Mind you, I believe the Rabaud was an excellent wine, rich and round and lusciously golden. It is classified as a first growth of Sauternes. And now, not for the first time, I was beginning to feel a little worried about Château Yquem. A bottle of old Château Yquem had first aroused my interest in wine, and Johnny's, about seven years ago. We had not drunk it often since then, usually only as a dessert wine, but we had kept our illusions about it; and strangely enough, Rosemary, too, had begun her education on Château Yquem.

. . . The sort of actor-manager you had fallen in love with while still at school. . . . " You won't like him so much in ten years' time, my child! " Indignant repudiation — but they were right; oh, they were right! I didn't. I don't. The sort of poetry, passionate, erotic, pierrotic — Stephen Phillips's *Paolo and Francesca,* for instance — which in your early youth had flushed the world rose-red for you, and clanged in your ear with a sound of silver clarions: " Have you tried re-reading it lately? " " No — but " — confidently — " I will! " and I did. It was awful.

So that I wondered a little uneasily about Château Yquem. . . .

Meanwhile the affable chambermaid was chat-

ting to Rosemary about the wines. " They are good —
yes? M. Garosse " — M. Garosse was the unknown
gentleman — " M. Garosse was puzzled at first, not
knowing the company, which wines to choose; and
then he said: ' *Puisqu'il y a des dames* . . . ' "
  " *Puisqu'il y a des dames.*"
  Because of the ladies!
  It did not need the rolling eyes of hatred which
Humphrey and Johnny both turned upon us for Rosemary and myself to explode into fury. We just waited
until the chambermaid departed. " *Puisqu'il y a des
dames* — " the old story, the old idiot fallacy that the
ladies preferred sweet wine. Why should we prefer
sweet wine? Has not a woman eyes, organs, dimen-
sions, senses, affections, passions, even as a man has?
And have we not palates, intelligence, taste, subtlety,
and a fastidious discrimination — even as a man has?
But there is a masculine type who will always classify
the ladies — God bless 'em! — as a form of kittle-
cattle who must be humoured and indulged, given compliments, lies, and sweetmeats, relegated to the drawing-room to gossip or to fuss, to read pretty novels or to
show off their frocks to an envious rival in frocks; and
that sums up the ladies, God bless 'em! So let's open

a bottle of Sauterne, Sigalas-Rabaud 1922. . . . That'll please 'em. And so to the serious business of life.

— By this time, when we had exhausted ourselves in repudiating our responsibility for the sweet wine, a responsibility which obviously rested entirely with M. Garosse's too easy conviction that all he heard about ladies was true, we were informed that M. Garosse's chauffeur was waiting to take us round the châteaux. Perhaps M. Garosse himself was a legend, for we never saw him. He remained a mysterious presence, dimly moving in the background, ordering our lives for that one day alone; and behind him M. Calvet moved; and behind M. Calvet? Was there anything still more virile and godlike and competent? I believe not.

At all events, the chauffeur, a nice plump sloe-eyed little man, having received his orders that we should be shown the vineyards of Sauternes, had determined that he would not be accused of a lack of zeal in performance of his duty. We *were* shown the vineyards of Sauternes, and the châteaux of Sauternes, and the cellars of Sauternes. . . .

I must mention here that this day of September 23rd was the hottest which had yet blazed down upon us on all the tour. It was hotter even than at Hermitage. I must mention, too, that as the chauffeur placed himself in front of our car, in order to guide Humphrey, who was driving, Johnny, Rosemary, and I were squeezed in behind. It was our fault that we had too many cloaks with us that day. It had been the sort of hot day which begins in mist, and might equally well have resulted in cold. I must mention, too, that we had finished those two bottles of Sauterne, because, thinking ourselves the guests of M. Garosse, backed by M. Calvet, backed by Jehovah, we were neither brave enough nor impolite enough to leave any! The affable chambermaid would doubtless have reported our actions and reactions. So that we set off for Château Yquem, that grand first growth of Sauternes, feeling already hot, sweet, and sticky; also with an uneasy longing upon us to turn our backs on the sort of afternoon that this was bound to be, and go and lie down somewhere, in a quiet, dim, and shadowy limbo.

Nevertheless, the first sight of Château Yquem brought its rewarding thrill, for this was really a château, not just a house; a beautiful old castle, with towers and big ceremonial gates, and an incredibly deep and ancient well in the central courtyard. While we were looking fearfully down the black hole of the well, through an archway at the far end of the courtyard appeared one of the smallest men I have ever seen, with enormous fierce white moustaches, and kind, childlike blue eyes. He looked like the Generalissimo of the Gnome Army. This was M. Daret, the steward at Château Yquem. Delightfully hospitable and witty he proved to be, and not at all averse from a certain quaint notoriety which his personality had earned for him among visitors to the romantic château. He made us sign our names in the visitors' book, where King Alphonso and Mr. Winston Churchill — these two especially — had already signed theirs; and then he invited us to sample the wine of three different years from the wood, '23, '24, '25.

Feeling rather faint and heavy, we straggled outside into the sunshine again, and down the steep bank which led to the vineyards. There the *vendangeuses* were already picking; they were very coy with Johnny when he tried to photograph them at their picturesque job, and dodged and scuffled round the vines, pretending that they were not worthy of the honour. Meanwhile the General of the Gnome Army

GROUP—WITHOUT JOHNNY—AT CHÂTEAU YQUEM

CHÂTEAU MARGAUX
THE BEST VINEYARD IN THE WORLD

showed us the dried grapes left hanging on their stalks, to grow sweeter and sweeter, and rotten-sweet, until they were like raisins with just one single drop of juice left in each centre.

The picking that was going on now was called the *trie;* that is to say, a sort of decimation, for only about every tenth grape had hung long enough to be ready. They have to be left until a sort of fungus, called Botrytis, produces the grey mould on them which is the very essence of Sauternes.

As we drove away from Château Yquem, I noticed, though my sense of beauty was rapidly becoming submerged and sleepy, that at the end of each row of vines a rose-bush grew and was in bloom.

The chauffeur told us, with vicarious pride, that the wines of Sauternes, *vins liquoreux,* sweet and rich and golden, gracious, mellow, and swooning, would never have existed but for an accident and M. Garosse's grandfather. It was in 1847, ten years after our good Queen Victoria came to the throne, that M. Garosse's grandfather noticed that a portion of his vineyard had been left too long unharvested, and that the grapes lay shrivelled and rotten, most of them, on the ground. Perhaps the weather had been unfavourable, or perhaps he had been away, and . . . At all events, there the grapes lay useless, which had hitherto been plucked at their normal season, and made into ordinary wine; good, plain, inconspicuous white wine; dry, perhaps; dry, not sweet. M. Garosse's grandfather could not bear waste. Sharply he ordered even these grapes to be gathered up and pressed out. That barrel could be set aside for the least among his labourers. And that barrel, *Messieurs et Mesdames,* that marvel of a wine, sweet, rich, and golden, was tasted by the Emperor of all the Russias on his tour through Europe, and he bought it for a fabulous sum! So that the haphazard discovery established a precedent; year after year all the owners of the vineyards of Sauternes allowed their grapes to grow, not only ripe, but rotten.

And we, uttering lip-service to this marvellous discovery, this joy, this miracle, this boon of mankind, swore softly, meanwhile, in our souls, at M. Garosse's grandfather, and at the Emperor of all the Russias, and at that fatal year 1847, in which vineyards which might have produced wine fit for gentlemen to drink — ay, and even for ladies, God bless 'em! — produced instead this clinging, highly perfumed, luscious, and full-blooded horror known as the great wine of Sauternes!

. . . I think that after this we must have all been too sullen with warmth and sweetness to put up any resistance to the will of the chauffeur of M. Garosse. I could not count how many châteaux we visited in that smiling region, nor how many sweet wines we sampled. There was Château Vignan, Château Filhot, Château Latour Blanche. . . . I believe, to the eternal credit of three of us, at least, that Rosemary and I still succeeded in paying the recurring Simon the Cellarer his meed of compliment, as we sampled his 1924 and 1925 of sticky new wine; and that Johnny still succeeded each time in twisting his face into something of a connoisseur's expression as he held his glass up to the light and drank. As for Humphrey, we missed him from these performances somewhere round about the fourth château after Château Yquem. . . . And found him sitting by the car, pretending to examine something in its inside, and asserting cantankerously that as far as Sauternes went: " I'm sunk! "

The rays of the sun grew ever hotter, our cloaks heavier, our skins stickier, and the chauffeur of M. Garosse ever more cheerful and implacable. . . .

" Next," he cried merrily, " we will visit Château Rieussec. They will let us taste their wine. It is of a very good quality. After that, Château d'Arche. You can see it from here if you stand up! " And obediently we tried to stand up.

The nightmare reached its epitome at Latour Blanche, where, just in front of the entrance to the cellars of that noble beverage, Humphrey was unable to start up the car. Something had gone wrong. There was no doubt but that here we were to remain for ever, stuck fast in the very heart and core of Sauternes; and waves of warm, sickly hopelessness flowed over us as again and again he cranked up the engine, and in vain. Presently, we imagined, the hospitable Simon the Cellarer and his wife would step out, seeing our plight, and beg us to come in and sit down, and eat and drink with them, and remain the night; and we should be given Sauternes for tea and for dinner and for breakfast and for ever. . . . We talked, in low, subdued voices, about the niceness of vinegar and sharp apples and olives and anchovies, and tried to keep up our spirits in that way, as we sat stuck together like three pear-drops at the back of the car which would not go.

. . . And in about half an hour it did go, and

we drove away from Château Latour Blanche, and away from Sauternes, and back to Langon, where, with many thanks and an adequate tip, we dropped M. Garosse's chauffeur; and then we drove away from Langon, and still farther away from Sauternes, along the road to Saint-Émilion. And the sun was setting, and there was a tang of autumn coolness in the air, and plenty of room in the car; and the scenery was unexpectedly exhilarating, and the plum-coloured bloom of evening lay upon the hills; and we were going towards a dinner at Libourne where we could choose the wine ourselves — dry wine, *vin sec,* not *demi-sec,* but *sec, sec, sec!*

XVII
SAINT-ÉMILION

WITH that hopefulness which would so gladly have stage-managed a royal climax to our day of anguish, we ordered a bottle of old Château Margaux to drink with our dinner at the hotel at Libourne . . . and were badly let down again. It was absolutely without bouquet and without body; not only indifferent, but evil. Now was the proprietor's chance — for we asked his opinion on it — to make the *beau geste;* to substitute a bottle of his best Saint-Émilion for the useless, tasteless Château Margaux, and so cancel the disgrace from our memories. However, he had not the wit to do that, nor the princely disposition. He merely stood at our table and talked too much, very politely and with every endeavour to please. He stood at our table for hours, talking, and when he finally succeeded, with difficulty, in moving himself away — "There are two things," quoth Humphrey, succinctly "of which the art of living rightly consists: first in learning *not* to be a nuisance, and then *when* to be a nuisance. Our friend has not yet learnt the first lesson; and we, obviously, have not yet learnt the second, or we should have made the hell of a fuss about this bottle being corked."

"Instead of just being plaintive about it," Johnny agreed. "Yes, I know, but my spirit is broken where claret is concerned."

I did not chime in with Johnny, over this. Prouder than ever was I in my allegiance to Bordeaux; prouder than ever, as failure piled upon failure gave it more and more the appearance of a lost cause. I have already spoken of my secret love of rant. Now, secretly, so that none should hear me, my soul was ranting like mad. . . . Up with the banner of Bordeaux! — And if, in Burgundy, every bottle that was brought to us should prove peerless and flawless, still, as Humphrey and Rosemary waxed more triumphant, still I should cling the more obdurately to my faith. Yes, and if all the world turned Burgundian (by this time I had practically lapsed into blank verse) — still would I remain a disciple of Bordeaux!

. . . But the Château Margaux at Libourne was really foul.

Our actions were still being guided by M. Calvet's iron hand in its velvet glove. We drove to Saint-Émilion next morning, only a short distance away, to keep an appointment with yet another unknown at the Hôtel des Gourmets — an excellently provocative name for a hotel!

Saint-Émilion is a beautiful little ramparted town, mainly of the thirteenth century. It revealed itself, on this glorious and rather crisp morning of late September, as a fascinating untidy medley of thick broken walls, stone archways, and lanes so steep that they were almost vertical, which suddenly broadened into terraces, whence you might look down on more ruins, more walls and archways and grey old towers. Our guide, a brisk and business-like young employee from a firm of wine-merchants in Bordeaux — " alert " and " zealous " are the adjectives with which an advertisement of a business-training college would have praised him — took us straight off to Château Ausone.

The cellars here were unlike any others we had ever seen, being carved amazingly out of the living rock; for this was a genuinely old château, and had taken its name from the Roman poet Ausonius, who is known to have had a vineyard in the Bordeaux country towards the end of the fourth century — though in all probability it was some miles away from Château Ausone.

The vineyards did not lie spread like an ocean outside the castle walls, as in the Médoc region. You found little bits of vineyard everywhere, mixed up with the ramparts and the bastions and the moats; and even when you climbed up and up the crumbling steps to where the old chapel and graveyard used to be, here unexpectedly was another small vineyard, drawing up its strength and juiciness from the earth where men had lain buried. Inside the little grey chapel of Château Ausone, high above Saint-Émilion, was a great heap of bones, bleached to white purity. They had been flung there by those who had dug up the cemetery to make a vineyard; and some cheery-looking skulls grinned at us brightly from the deeper shadows.

One patch of ungrafted French vines was still left at Château Ausone, of the pre-phylloxera period. The vines were more than a hundred years old. They did not bear grapes any more, but the proprietor's sense of romance still allowed them to twist their gnarled woody stems into fantastic shapes, uncut and unmolested.

The best years of Château Ausone, we were informed, are 1900, 1904, 1906, 1911, and 1914; or, if you wish to lay down in the wood, 1924. The present proprietor, M. Dubois, still has some bottles of 1831, but they would taste, I should imagine, like the ghost of a great wine, and the flavour could be but a mere whisper. One of the best wine-merchants from whom to order Château Ausone is M. Eschenauer, Allé de Boutant, Bordeaux.

Returning again to Saint-Émilion, very much impressed with what we had seen, we noticed how the proud inhabitants had placarded their walls with trumpetings and swagger: " *Saint-Émilion! Ses Remparts! Ses Monuments Monolithes! Ses Vins! Ses Macarons!* " Sometimes " *Ses Macarons!* " appeared alone. Discarding for the moment the monoliths, we decided in favour of the wine and macaroons; that is to say, we went to our lunch at Les Gourmets, where, we were told by the nice plump proprietor and his plump pretty daughter, M. Calvet himself frequently lunched, and loved their special *pommes-de-terre sautées*. It was a very good lunch indeed, ending with two delicious *spécialités:* tiny, milk-white, circular macaroons; and little blood-peaches; that is to say, peaches dyed, flesh and skin, as deep a crimson as a blood-orange.

As for our wines, we had a procession; for the Simon-the-Cellarer at Château Ausone had given us a bottle of 1924 to take back to our lunch; and we drank this second, after the *vin ordinaire*. Third in sequence came a bottle of Château Petit Faurie Souchard 1911, which is a most excellent Saint-Émilion, not very well known as yet, but deserving a wider appreciation. Finally we had a bottle of Château Trimoulet 1906, which, however, was a good deal more fiery than the 1911, and was emphatically the sort of wine that could have idled away another ten years in the cellar, before, at the age of thirty or thereabouts, it was brought up into daylight. It was made from *vieux ceps* grapes; that is to say, from the old French pre-phylloxera vines.

After this, and remembering Sauternes, we felt rather disinclined to visit any more châteaux, where we should most likely be hospitably invited to taste new wines from the wood; so we went instead to visit the troglodyte church of the eleventh century, hewn out of the rock, like a vast cave. Here they still hold a service once a year, on the Sunday after All Saints' Day. The altar of Saint Émilion is surmounted by a rough carving, showing two giant bottles with flame emerging from the necks; and over the principal altar is another carving, supposed to be of Saint Michael and the dragon; but it is difficult in the crumbling stone to distinguish figures clearly. Johnny, indeed, who believed the church to be very much older than its purported eleventh-century origin, had a theory that this was a prehistoric carving, of approximately the same date as the Altamira wall-paintings in Spain. It is his idea that the carving represents a man and an elk, and that the so-called dragon is in reality a primitive attempt to show an elk running, with its horns springing backwards from its head.

Amid all the welter of historical discussion which ensued between Johnny and Humphrey, who had found in Saint-Émilion a bountiful playground, monolithic, troglodytic, prehistoric, Roman, mediæval, and Girondin, I drew a little away; rested against one of the massive, giant pillars that marched in severe simplicity down each side of the nave, and thought, first, how they reminded me of the church of San-

Paolo-fuori-le-mura in, or rather outside, Rome; and secondly, how curiously incongruous our little friend, M. Calvet's representative, looked, leaning up against an opposite pillar, well dressed, dapper, obliging . . . down here in the rock and darkness, where there was no one to dress for, no one to be dapper for, no one actually for the moment to oblige. He did not seem definitely bored, only astonished to be where he was, and not quite sure how it had happened. His instructions were, of course, to stick to us like death, but doubtless the iron hand had not anticipated that we would leave the châteaux, and go groping back into the eleventh century, instead.

We went down, next, into the cell of Saint Émilion, where that noble hermit, with the insatiable arrogance and exhibitionism of all hermits, had made himself as uncomfortable as possible, and then had sat there meekly awaiting the constant arrival of pilgrims to see him *being* uncomfortable. Here, again carved into the living rock, was his hard chair, his hard bed, all in the underground gloom; his spring of pure water, which still pauses in a pool like black looking-glass, and then rushes on below the stone and below the earth to feed all the present town of Saint-

Émilion. In the pool under the hermit's cell, if you gaze down into it, you can see a welter of heaped-up silver, sharply gleaming. The little girl whose candle guided us through those ruins told us that these were pins, cast two and two, by maidens on the saint's own day. If the pins fall crossed, the maiden who flings them marries within the year.

The famous cellars of the Clos des Cordeliers are built into the old monastery. We went through broken cloisters, with no roof but the sky; narrow, delicate arches slicing the sunshine, the pillars so frail that I felt they might snap between my fingers. A bird called the tree-creeper suddenly scuttled up one of the tall trees, justifying its name. Then we plunged down a passage, and more and more passages, steeply descending, crystallizing the mental image I have always had of Francis Thompson flying from the Hound of Heaven:

> I fled Him, down the nights and down the days;
> I fled Him, down the arches of the years. . . .

There was an occasional, very occasional, gleam of light; the vaults overhead had dripped into sharp stalactites. In the very bowels of the earth we found pale handsome boys, coping with strange machinery, to the sound of dull thuddings and thumpings. Actually and fantastically, they were making the wine sparkle, for all the Clos des Cordeliers is *mousseux*. The cold down in these vaults bit and stung; so that when I had been a few seconds out again in the blazing sunshine, I felt like an *omelette surprise*.

We sat out in the cloisters for a little while, and shared a bottle of Clos des Cordeliers with our dapper guide and one of the pale boys. It was *demi-sec*, and might very well have been Champagne, excepting for the difference in price. The price, I believe, was about twelve francs; and night-clubs might do worse than buy up enormous consignments, and pour it into their labelled but empty Champagne bottles. Probably they do!

We took back with us to our hotel at Libourne a bottle of Curé Bon, procured for us, with a certain amount of difficulty, by our efficient guide, who had heard me express a capricious desire to taste it. I was really basing my sudden fancy entirely on the name. Curé Bon had a pleasant smack to it. One saw the good *curé* — Parson Good his name was, translated! — with his own little vineyard and his thirsty flock, busily, contentedly, and thriftily making his own wine, and marvelling when he woke one day to find it was famous. I had seen the funny little square house, with the sign " Curé Bon " above the front door, standing stolid and solitary among its vines. It had the right sort of legendary smack to it — not twilit Celtic legend, but the practical French kind, containing food and drink and a table-cloth, and stating clearly how old everybody is. Curé Bon . . . But they told me that unwittingly I had made a most fastidious selection. Curé Bon was a very distinguished first growth of Saint-Émilion; and some even ranked it on a level with Château Ausone. We all four liked it immensely, and reckoned it a discovery. Curé Bon de la Madeleine was its full name, 1918, very clear and still. I should like to lay down a good supply, if it will age well.

Our hotel deserves mention for the fact that it was the only one we had yet encountered where mosquito-nets were provided for the beds; we had suffered a fair amount from mosquitoes ever since we left Avignon. Also, the staff were particularly charming; we knew they would be, from the moment we saw the wall-eyed chambermaid. We were to be looked after, at various hostelries, by three wall-eyed cham-

bermaids, and each one of the three was capable,
warm-hearted, and willing. It may be that their parents
had told them at birth that because of their misfortune
they must make themselves beloved in other ways. . . .

But at dinner that second night at Libourne,
we gave the Bordeaux region its last chance, and in a
spirit of desperate defiance ordered a bottle of 1887
Latour, not château-bottled, but still, perhaps . . .
Perhaps, and maybe, and yet-might-it-be-possible . . .

— Rosemary shook her head. " Rather poor! "
was her verdict. " It makes my tongue feel as though
it had been sandpapered! "

And Humphrey did not say a word.

XVIII
VOUVRAY AND *TERRINES*

THE weather and the landscape that we passed through on the first stage of our northward journey from Libourne to Burgundy was autumn and spring whimsically entangled, crisp as autumn, and languid as spring; pear-trees and lilac actually in bloom, contrasted with patches of tall Jerusalem artichokes in yellow flower, with Indian corn and dahlias and scarlet salvias, dabbling the quiet blue sky with bright colour; and shining pomegranate-trees that arched their boughs of gold-copper fruit over most of the cottage doorways. An occasional baby château, with miniature towers, completed the peaceful pattern of the tapestry.

We were surprised to hear that Jerusalem artichokes are not looked on as a delectable food, in France. The roots are given to beasts, or made into alcohol for hairwash!

We lunched at the Grand Hôtel de France, Chalais. Let no one be misled by the pompous name. It was a very small inn, trees planted close about it; and a long, narrow dining-room, with a wooden floor, and one set of knives and forks to be used for all the courses. Our meal, which was served us by an extraordinarily deft and pretty girl, was typical of what one may expect in almost any small place in France; not of the trout-and-partridge grade, but just below it, where they shyly suggest omelet and veal, and you take it for granted that these will be well cooked and quickly dished up; and that, in addition, there will be hors-d'œuvres, vegetables, cheese, fruit, and coffee. We drank *vin ordinaire*, a really good light white wine, with a rounded flavour; and the bill for the four of us, including all these things, and probably four vermouths and a couple of *fines*, amounted to seventy-six francs — about nine shillings.

That lunch was a pleasant memory; and so was our arrival towards evening, at Angoulême, at the Nouvel Hôtel des Trois Piliers, where we were received in the joyful spirit of an old nurse welcoming back her bairns after twenty years, when they are grown men and women. We had sent a wire, announcing that we intended to spend a night there; so, according to previous request, they had prepared *homard thermidor* for three of us, and delicious fried soles for one — the one being myself. I have never really cared for lobster since, in Cornwall, I went lobster-glotto! The outposts of the meal, at either end, were our old friends, that excellent white *vin ordinaire*, and the 1873 Cognac, which should be spoken of with bared head, and in a voice of reverence. But in between we drank a bottle of Château Latour 1918 — a very promising wine, but young, and therefore crude in the after-taste. In twenty years, perhaps . . .

But meanwhile: " Not *very* good, dear, I'm afraid," said Rosemary, gently. Humphrey said never a word. . . .

> — *Es ist eine alte Geschichte,*
> *Doch bleibt sie immer neu;*
> *Und wem sie just passieret,*
> *Dem bricht das Herz entzwei!*

Our lunch the next day, at Saint-Jean-d'Angely, in contrast to the lunch at Chalais, was most sinister: we had to drive the car up a long, cobbled alley; and directly we stopped, a hag, grey and thin and angry, rushed out from one of the doorways, and began mopping and mowing, and making wide-flung melodramatic gestures of despair, reminding us of what Sybil Thorndike would have been, in the part of any Dumb Old Woman, at the Guignol. However, as there seemed no other spot to park the car, we had to ignore Dumb Old Woman, who, with one final fatalistic gesture of her skinny arms, sweeping us downwards and away, out of all luck and light, disappeared again under the arch of her doorway, next to the hotel.

The dining-room at the hotel was sinister, too. Those who waited upon us were silent and joyless, their movements mechanical, their eyes sullen. Lunch was almost uneatable, and the only literally bright spot in it was quite an agreeable *vin rosé*.

But the outside world was a compensation, for no gloom could last long on that cold, brilliant autumn day. Thouars, where we had arranged to spend that first night of our northward journey to Burgundy, proved to be a small ramparted town, standing solitary on a hill. It was there, at the Hôtel du Cheval Blanc on the very crest of the hill, that we tasted, at dinner, our first Vouvray: a Château Moncontour 1920; I think, from later experience, that this is the only dry Vouvray. I had heard much of this wine, having been told that it was wonderful when drunk in its own region, and utterly unlike any other wine; so that we took our first sip with keen curiosity.

Its bouquet, certainly, was distinctive. Humphrey said it reminded him of wet iron. I have never noticed the bouquet of wet iron, but I cannot imagine that it has anything like the delicate crispness of Vouvray. Vouvray tastes more like Rhine wine than French. I know of no better wine to encourage a mood of gay exhilaration. In this it is like really lilting waltz music, not heavy, mawkish, melancholy waltzes, but Schubert, Johann Strauss, Lehar, and Fall. Wine gaiety should halt, laughing, just on the brink of intoxication. I remember a wine in Italy which induced this evanescent happiness, this rapture with all things, not as they were, but as I, for the moment, thought them. It was called Soave Veronese; and I drank it, most appropriately, sitting outside a café, opposite the amphitheatre at Verona, on a blazing September day. It was not an elfin, elusive white wine, like Vouvray; but crimson, and mellow, and, as its name indicates, suave.

. . . Presently I found myself swaggering down an arcade in Verona, with watch-shops on either side of me. I had never seen so many beautiful watches. The Arcade of the Jewelled Watches! — it sounded as romantic as the Street of Swords in Toledo. I vowed, then, that when I was richer — not if, but *when,* for I was confident with Soave Veronese — I would return here and buy a watch. Two years later a friend of mine was going to Verona, and, being then " in purse," I commissioned her to buy me a watch. I described to her the arcade, with watch-shops one beside the other for the whole length and on either side. " You can't miss it! " I said — but it transpired that she could. There was, indeed, no arcade entirely composed of watchmongers in all Verona. It did not exist. She could not even find so many as two watch-shops side by side. She bought for me quite a pretty little watch, the sort that you can easily find in any jeweller's in any town of a certain size. . . . But I had been happy in an arcade in Verona, I had drunk Soave Veronese, and walked with the gods, and on either side of me were watch-shops, thousands of watch-shops, millions of watches, all gloriously ticking away the vermilion hours. . . .

Funny thing, wine! A mere germ that creeps into and foments the juice of a grape, and then . . .

" It's a good thing God thought of it," said Humphrey,
one day; " because *I* shouldn't have! "

So that night, after dinner, at Thouars, instead
of feeling, as we usually did, lumpish and sleepy from
our day of fast driving and rushing air, we felt joyful
and enterprising; and went swinging out to explore,
down the hill, through the town, and on to the ramparts. It was a night of black velvet, with cold flashing
stars, and Thouars felt like mediæval France. Somehow we found ourselves thinking of the fine old names
that once embroidered the map — Acquitaine, Gascony, Touraine. . . . Of old wars, too! Of archers
and the first cannons. We walked round the tower of
the Black Prince, where he had sojourned for some
months during his victories in France; and I remembered learning about him from *Little Arthur's History
of England,* and being bidden to admire him for his
infernally priggish act in bringing home the captive
King John on a great white horse, while he himself
rode meekly beside him on a small pony. Even as a
child, it had struck me that the Black Prince would
have been nicer still if he had allowed King John to
remain somewhere in quiet obscurity, instead of drag-
ging him through the streets, conspicuous on an im-

mense charger. Viewed from an adult and psychological standpoint, it is, of course, quite obvious that our modest Black Prince was an adept at stage-managing himself effectively.

. . . Presently, scrambling up and down steep cobbled lanes, past dark entries that led we knew not whither, we passed under an archway that was certainly one of the old gates of the town, and found ourselves on the walls, with the road running below, and the fortifications like cliffs behind us.

Old wars . . . old magic. . . . The air was like black wine. We could only dimly see each other's faces. Suddenly, among the ruins, above or below us, you could hardly tell which, came heavy steps, then the crumbling and sliding of stones . . . steps again, whispering, and silence. A sentry, maybe, had left his post for a few minutes for a kiss from Mademoiselle, who had slipped away from her father's vigilance. But he should be on duty. At any moment the English archers might attack. . . .

Well, these were old wars.

Our journey the next day was through what is known as the château country. By unspoken consent we did not enter a single one of the famous castles, though we passed Chinon, and Loche, Loudain, Tours, and finally Amboise, where we slept that night; but somehow we felt that a wine-tour would be rather overloaded if it actually involved getting out of the car and taking an intelligent interest in the insides of some seven or eight castles of different periods and centuries and histories. Besides, seeing each great château, first as a shape on the skyline, high on a hill, or washed by the river; drawing nearer and nearer; and then just not alighting, is a distinct sensation of its own, not without pleasure — the perverse pleasure, I suppose, which lies in missed opportunities.

Humphrey was smoking Wills' Gold Flake cigarettes at that time, which contained in each packet a picture from the Famous Châteaux series; and he held firmly to the opinion that this was the least exhausting and the most satisfactory way of "doing" the châteaux. I am afraid it is quite evident that the leading characteristic of our quartet was laziness —

Lazy — I want to be lazy . . .
I want to be out in the sun
With no work to be done,
Under that awning
They call the sky. . . .

And " under that awning they call the sky " we sat at Vouvray, in the garden of the Hôtel du Pont de Cisse, drinking Château Moncontour again, *très sec*, 1920; an exquisitely luxurious sensation. It was a pale Chablis, greenish-gold, and the rhythm of our happy mood danced down on us again, and carried us buoyantly through the day. Rosemary, who sometimes drove the car, now drove it, after drinking Vouvray, as though it were the only car in the world on the only road, confidently, carelessly, and singing as she drove. . . .

We lunched at Chinon, on the River Vienne, and drank Grand Vin de Chinon, Clos d'Argenson, a pleasant, light, but undistinguished wine. But the Castle of Chinon I shall remember always, with its long greyhound lines, high above the river; the most lovely and legendary of all the châteaux. The massive strength of Loudain, with walls so thick that it seemed nothing could overthrow them, with moat, portcullis, and drawbridge, in all the best traditions of castle fame and castle legends, was, in its own way, as impressive. Chinon had slipped out from between the pages of the Book of Old, Old French Fairy-Tales; but Loudain we used to build out of sand, and it took a whole morning to build it strong enough to resist the incoming tide. . . .

Our way lay along the north bank of the Loire, a wide unemotional river with many shallows and islands; and we were puzzled by the curious troglodytic houses, like caves, built into the cliff, lower than the road, and lower, it seemed, than the river, between Saint-Mars, Lapille, and Tours, as far as Vouvray. It was as though a race of dwarfs had burrowed their dwelling here, preferring the semi-darkness.

The château at Amboise was far too ornate and over-decorated to be beautiful; and, moreover, an atmosphere of char-à-bancs hung all about it. We crossed the bridge on to the south bank, and went to the excellent Hôtel de France et Cheval Blanc, where the view, the food, and the staff were all full of charm; and Johnny discovered an excellent quality of wolf-dog — though not quite as good as the one at Thouars, he said; and indeed she had been a little darling at Thouars, almost as graceful and capricious as our own Tessa, left behind in Italy.

At Thouars we had all been very stupid; for there they kept a fox-cub unhappily in a cage, and we had longed to kidnap it, and carry it away in a sack, and let it run free and wild again in the green and russet rich-smelling woods that we passed on today's run. We had only *not* stolen it and carried it off in this arbitrary fashion because of the difficulties that had naturally arisen from the entire staff of a hotel, including the proprietor, and half the village, standing round in the courtyard to wave us farewell. But now that it was too late, now that we were already in Amboise, and a day's swift travel away, it occurred to us that we could quite simply and honestly have *bought* the fox-cub. They would surely have sold it to us, rejoicing, for less than a hundred francs; and then we could have seen it plunge into the undergrowth and vanish like a red-brown streak, never, perhaps, to be caught again — at all events, not without a run for it. It is curious that the honest method of acquiring it did not first occur to us!

With our dinner, at Amboise, we drank a wine we had never yet heard of, a Saint Nicholas Bourgeuil, 1921; here in the Loire region they export very little, and the wine-lists are exciting and unfamiliar. Saint Nicholas Bourgeuil was a good drink, clear ruby colour, soft and pleasant to the palate. We followed it up by a Vouvray 1893 — thirty-three years is a good age, and we did not mind that this veteran was slightly sweet, for we drank it as a dessert wine; it was a sparkling, rich deep gold, mellow in flavour, and with plenty of character.

If, when you lunch at the Hôtel de l'Écu de Bretagne, at Beaugency, the *maître d'hôtel* should prove to be busy and bad-tempered, should he domineer over your wishes with terrifying bursts of *" Sapristi! "* and *" Nom d'un chien! "* — remember always that he is a lamb with a lion's moustache; for if I had found this out at the beginning, instead of at the end, of our most succulent lunch, I should not have sat quaking and apologetic, from the vermouth to the *fine*.

It was, as a matter of fact, the vermouth which began the trouble. The *maître d'hôtel*, when we entered, was charging about among his beseeching clients like an enraged but confident bull who has learnt not to break the china. . . . These zoological comparisons will occur! I must say for the man, however, that he did not keep us waiting. *" Quatre vermouths français! "* we said, quickly, for he made no attempt to conceal, as he stood by our table, that he was chafing to be off again. In a flash he was back, arranged the glasses, poured out half a vermouth — *"Pah!"* No! The bottle was finished; these were the dregs. Impatiently he substituted another bottle, pulled the cork, poured out four vermouths. . . . Then suddenly and suspiciously raised the bottle to his nose, shook his head, muttered an oath, swept away the four full glasses and the bottle, and disappeared.

Before we had had much time to speculate on the meaning of this, he reappeared with yet another bottle, and four more glasses. This time he seemed satisfied. Humphrey, however, was not.

"Esker c'est vermouth français?" he asked, in that style of French which will for ever maintain the reputation of the Englishman abroad.

The *maître d'hôtel* glared at him. *"Vermouth italien!"* he rapped back.

"S'il vous plaît," said our slow and imperturbable Humphrey, *" s'il vous plaît, nong. Vermouth français!"*

. . . I do not care to remember in detail that panic-stricken moment, though it is easy to divine that Johnny's hand, under the table, had stolen swiftly to his hip-pocket. . . . The *maître d'hôtel* seemed to gather himself as for some mighty explosion; but

" *Sapr—r—risti!* " was all he growled; " *Ça m'énerve à la fin!* "

" *Nous aimong,*" intrepid Humphrey went on, " *vermouth français. Pas italien. Trop dooss. Français!* "

— The *maître d'hôtel* went away. He returned with a bottle of *vermouth français;* Noilly Pratt, in fact, which we always preferred, as an *apéritif,* by itself, though Italian vermouth is necessary to mix in cocktails. He also brought four more glasses. He poured out the Noilly, and left us to drink it. . . .

"Have you read *The Virginian?* " asked Johnny of the rest of us, reminiscently. " There's a wonderful bit in it about a cow-boy who went into a small restaurant, where he was handed a menu including all sorts of delicacies, among them being ' Frogs' Legs *à la* Delmonico,' which the cow-boy ordered. The proprietor of the restaurant then produced two revolvers, which he pointed at the cow-boy, saying: ' *You'll 'ave 'ash!* ' "

" You'll 'ave *terrine!* " — or words to that effect, said the *maître d'hôtel,* reappearing suddenly before us.

We did 'ave *terrine.* If *terrine* rhymed with

" dream," I would make a poem about it. It was " *terrine de la maison*," and, as the chef afterwards told me, the main ingredients were crushed partridges. We ranked it, with the *brandade* at Avignon, the *cêpes bordelais* at Bordeaux, and the *pâté de lièvre* at Châteauneuf-du-Pape, as one of the great culinary experiences of our tour. Timidly, oh, but very timidly, I whispered something of this to the *maître d'hôtel* when he came round again with the dish. He seemed slightly mollified, and, almost without pausing in his stride, gave us each another large slice.

After the *terrine* came omelet, a beauty, served in a fiery sauce, licked by transparent blue flame. Then we had the tenderest Chateaubriand steak that France had as yet given me.

The wine was not quite up to the level of the food. We began with Cheverney 1919, a quite well-behaved white wine; and this was followed by a Beaugency *décanté*, 1921. The Beaugency might have been a very good wine indeed, had it not been so rigidly frozen that no flavour at all was perceptible. On a bright cold day, like this twenty-ninth of September, you do prefer your red wine to be somewhat *chambré*. Never has wine been so cuddled as was this

Beaugency by us in our efforts to unfreeze it. We treated it like an almost drowned kitten whom we were attempting to restore to life; but in spite of everything, the cold weather won, and we still do not know the taste of Beaugency 1921.

Resigned, we turned away from it to an eau-de-vie, very different from any other kind, with a strong bouquet, and a taste of schnapps.

The bill, when it was brought, proved that this extraordinarily good meal was also extraordinarily cheap.

Waiting while Humphrey brought the car round, I encountered the *maître d'hôtel* again, just outside the door. He was talking to the chef. The luncheon rush was over. He was smiling amiably; so was the chef, a meek little man in white linen, with a pointed beard. I went up to them, and faltered my compliments. The *maître d'hôtel* was very pleased. Encouraged, I went on to tell him how afraid I had been at the beginning of the meal. He patted my hand:

"*Mais non!* you must not be afraid of Papa — " (I forget his nickname — Papa something.) "What was there to be afraid of? I am very fond of the ladies, I!" And then followed a well-chosen compliment. He introduced me to the chef. The chef introduced me to the *terrine de la maison*. We all bowed, and approved of one another. The chef told me how many stars and decorations he had. I, in return, told him how many more I would give him had I the bestowal in my power. We were all very happy. I liked the Hôtel de l'Écu de Bretagne, at Beaugency.

Our good lunch, followed by four hours of high-speed motoring through the snapping, brilliant, cold afternoon, made us all drowsy. At sunset we saw the little, fortified town of Sancerre on the summit of a hill that was golden and red with vines. The hill stood up alone in a flat landscape of vines, all ruddy and autumn-coloured, and through it the white road looped and ran and lost itself again, and went up and up till it disappeared behind the topmost wall. Seen thus across the plains, Sancerre had all the silent enchantment of a scene worked on tapestry.

On an impulse, for we had meant to go as far as Pouilly-sur-Loire that night, we decided to mount that spiralling white road, up and up, to Sancerre.

It was a mistake, of course. Not a bad mistake. We found a reasonably comfortable hotel, and dined reasonably well. The wine of Sancerre is not particularly distinguished; though I believe it was here, at the Hôtel du Point du Jour et de l'Écu, that the proprietor brought out a really old vermouth which had lain a long time in wood, and a still longer time in bottle. Up till then, funnily enough, it had never occurred to me that vermouth would gain handsomely by the same respectful treatment that we accord to wine.

But never again, not that evening, nor the next morning, when we drove away again, nor from within the walls of the town, did Sancerre ever appear to us with the glamour of that moment when we first saw her, at sunset, on the hill, across the red-gold vineyards.

XIX
POUILLY–SUR–LOIRE

THE cold lashed us out of our beds early the next morning, and put us early on to the road. We had planned to stop at Pouilly-sur-Loire for a bottle of wine at the Hôtel Neuf, where Humphrey and Rosemary had sampled it the winter before.

But a bottle of wine, unaccompanied, seemed a chilly prospect at that hour of the morning, about ten-thirty a.m., too late for breakfast, too early for lunch. Just before we entered the little town, and quite suddenly — as genius will! — I achieved popularity.

"Let's have it with eggs and bacon!"

Thus, and as simply as that, do we make ourselves beloved among our fellow men. Humphrey and Rosemary and Johnny for the rest of the day spoke to me with a reverential caress in their voices.

We entered the cheerful hotel dining-room, its walls painted with amorous pierrots, and Rosemary asked Madame if she remembered them. Madame did, instantly. Nothing marvellous in such affirmation; it was part of her job. But then she went on to prove that she sincerely did remember them: " Monsieur and Madame were on their way to such and such a place. Madame wore . . . Monsieur said . . . " Really quite an amazing feat.

She took our order for four *œufs au plat* with *jambon grillé,* and for a bottle of the same Pouilly-sur-Loire which they already knew. We waited impatiently — until we read the following text, hanging on the wall among the pierrots: " *Pour bien manger, sachez attendre. Une bonne cuisine est le contraire d'une auto. Plus elle va lentement, meilleur elle est.*" Then we waited patiently.

I find it difficult to do sufficient justice to Pouilly-sur-Loire. Humphrey and Rosemary had undoubtedly been right in their enthusiasm, and they were greatly relieved to see how ardently Johnny and I agreed with them. It is a very lovely white wine, dry, and extraordinarily soft, with a most fragrant bouquet; it leaves a trail of dim golden silk across the palate. After the 1906 we tried a bottle of 1911, which was deeper in colour, but not quite so exquisite, and with more of a pronounced gun-flint flavour, recalling the Côte-du-Rhône wines. The proprietress of the Hôtel Neuf gladly answered all our questions about this treasure. It was made from Blanc Fumé grapes, and kept two years in wood. 1925 was a good year to lay down.

There are moments in your life, not of massive importance, not determining your future this way or that, elusive to catch, and still more elusive to describe, which are nevertheless so complete in their utter rightness — every small accessory settling down into its place without hitch or angularity — that you feel, remembering such moments, a glow of gratitude. Of such quality was this impromptu meal of ours at Pouilly-sur-Loire. Hardly a glittering or expensive meal; and the company round the table was the same that had sat round tables for the last three weeks, and would do so for the next fortnight. But the roads were hard and good, and the car was running well, and autumn was sharp with cold and gay with colour; the bacon and eggs were an inspiration, for we were hungry; the hotel dining-room was large and light and full of welcome; and the hotel itself was small, and equally full of welcome. And we were on our way to royal Burgundy, a word ringed with magic, panoply, and trumpets. So there was really nothing *not* to be happy about, as we sat there, drinking 1906 Pouilly-sur-Loire, which is a wine to make you feel as though you were in love for the first time!

XX
THE SLOPES OF GOLD

THE invisible Master of Ceremonies who directed our entrance into Burgundy was aware of the value of pageantry. In Bordeaux no one had been aware of it. There is a famous road which runs from Chagny to Dijon, and all along are planted the grand vineyards; most of the more royal growths of Burgundy lie on the further side of Beaune — Romanée-Conti, Richebourg, Clos de Vougeot; but as we licked up the superb stretch of reinforced concrete on the last lap of our journey, the names which flashed past from the low walls — Grand Auxey, Meursault, Pommard, Volnay, were familiar enough to excite us.

When we entered the Côte d'Or, the hills far ahead in the east were drenched and misted in fabulous hues of pale gold, so that they looked like a myth told about hills long ago; but to our right and left, where the sun had already withdrawn, the colour of the ranges had ebbed and ebbed, from flame to damson, and from deep warm damson to indigo. The vines, here in this more northern region, had already been well stung by the cold, and their leaves ran chromatically through all the yellows, bronzes, chestnuts, and dark purples of their final flaunting array before they wither and fall. I was envious of all this pomp for Burgundy. In this fashion, and no other, should the big vineyards of the world make their impression on pilgrims from a country which grows no wine.

Nearly everyone who goes to Beaune stays at the Hôtel de la Poste. Here, too, they understand skilful staging of their effects. The proprietor, or rather, as we afterwards discovered, the proprietor's son-in-law, came forward as we entered the dining-room, and asked us if we would dine well, or dine table d'hôte. When it was put to us like that, we rather naturally answered that we would dine well! He approved our decision, and murmured something about *poulet au Chambertin.* That did not sound bad. Then we asked for the wine-list, and Humphrey fell upon it; Johnny and I remaining suitably in the background on this occasion.

Being human beings and not angels, we were not altogether displeased at seeing a slight cloud of disappointment on Humphrey's brow. "There seems to be nothing older than 1919," he said, slowly. Rosemary called up the proprietor: "We wanted to consult you," she began charmingly, "about the wine —— " Here he rushed in before she had time to go any further. He told us that Burgundy was not the same as Bordeaux; and that it made a difference in wine which year you chose; also that one vintage differed in taste and flavour from another. . . .

"*Tiens?*" said Rosemary, a little piqued; and indeed it did seem as though the stamp of our recent studies and experiences should in some way be so marked upon us as to defend us from this sort of instruction. "*Mais nous sommes déjà un peu connoisseurs, vous savez.*"

We chose for ourselves a Chablis de Clos, 1919, with a Chambertin 1919 to follow. The latter was the proprietor's choice. He said it would go well with the *poulet au Chambertin.* The staging of the wines, here, at this hotel, and indeed everywhere in the region, was again infinitely superior to the casual habits of the Bordelais, who slung their most precious

wines about as though they were serving bottled lemon-
ade. Here, the wines were carefully warmed and
cradled, or, if necessary, iced, to exactly the right
degree, carried as though they were the Holy Grail,
and poured into gigantic tulip-shaped glasses with
reverent ceremonial. As a matter of fact, I thought
the glasses for the Chambertin were exaggeratedly immense. You had to tilt them practically upside down
before any of the liquid at the bottom could reach
your lips.

After the soup a gigantic fish was brought to
us, lying voluptuously full length on a dish. Its name
was *brochet meunière,* which translated itself as pike,
disguised by art and a glorious sauce. The Chablis
which we drank with this most excellent fellow brought
bubbling to the surface again all my dormant springs
of belief that Chablis was the best white wine in the
world; better than Montrachet; better than Rhone
wine, or either of the Pouillys; better than white Hermitage; and oh, how much better than Château Yquem!
This Chablis had that rare pale effect of shot green
and gold, and the fragrance and the flavour were unforgettable.

We had to wait a long time for our *poulet au*

Chambertin, but it was a monumental dish when it arrived, and it would take hours to tell of all the delicacies which we found in the gravy. As for the Chambertin itself, it is not among my favourite Burgundies. This 1919 had a wonderful bouquet of violets, but the taste lingered a long way behind.

I must mention a special cheese called Minstère, like Camembert, only better, which they gave us here, and which we could get nowhere else. It immensely improved the flavour of the wine. As for the *fine de la maison* 1858, which, in a breathless hush, was slowly poured into glasses so overwhelmingly huge that any of them could have been used as a rose-bowl in the centre of a mayoral banquet, that brandy was almost an anæsthetic in bouquet. I believe in glasses of this size, for brandy; you can slowly inhale the rising perfume, and enjoy all the voluptuous pleasure of reeling back from it, dazed and incredulous.

Altogether a not undistinguished meal.

The next morning we went to see M. Jaboulet-Vercherre, who owns the old Clos de la Commaraine vineyard, and is a grower of good wines both at Hermitage and at the Côte d'Or. His speciality is Pommard. He very charmingly invited us all to lunch on the following day. So on this day we lunched at the Hôtel Terminus, Beaune, where I much enjoyed a Corton 1915, its hue a very glorious red when you lifted it to the rays of the sun. The name on the label, however, reminded me of a rather inglorious episode in my past, when I had just begun to know a little, a very little indeed, about wine. A good friend of mine, a perfect hostess, who always treats her guests with the delicate forethought of a loyalist making the ex-king of a lost cause believe that he is worthy of even better entertainment than a reigning king, once gave me white Corton 1915. Ungratefully, for it was a most delicious wine, I chid her for the date, pointing out that 1915 had been a poor year for Burgundy, and it should have been 1914. . . . Well, I am older, and, fortunately, know less certainly about everything now than I did! That 1915 white Corton was a peerless wine. 1915 was the right year. I take this opportunity of apologizing to my hostess, with a promise that I will be less bumptious next time!

It speaks powerfully for the effect of the Burgundy wines on my sense of observation that I seem to recall nothing whatever of our stay at Beaune except our meals; with the exception, perhaps, of the eight dancing Siamese kittens, who lived with their Siamese parents in the pantry of the hotel, and who were continually darting out into the hall and dining-room, nimble as monkeys. Funny, fascinating little cats they were, with big blue eyes; their noses, ears, tails, and paws, sombre splashes of mud-colour. We were so entranced by the spectacle of these kittens, tumbling in and out of wine-cradles, or lying, when we would permit them, with Buddhist faces and crossed paws in the hollow of our necks, motionless for hours, that we bought two of the older litter, who were big enough to travel, and arranged for the proprietor to send them to us by train to Avignon, to reach us there on the day we left for home; for we did not fancy the idea of having the rest of our leisurely journeying accompanied day and night, in the car and out of it, by the imperious, angry miaowings of this particular breed of cat; their inflection was always more profane than sacred, and they clawfully resented the slightest attention being paid to anything but themselves.

There is an interesting theory, which our own experience inclines us to accept, that these cats used to be kept entirely in the Siamese harems. This is supposed to account for the fact that they are never quiet

had been served to us, the triumph of the Burgundians over the Bordelais had not been unbearable for Johnny and myself.

Humphrey and Rosemary were beginning to look bothered.

XXI
LUNCHEON WITH A VINTNER

ROSEMARY was the only one of our quartet not to be surprised when our hospitable host, M. Jaboulet-Vercherre, and his extremely pretty wife, gave us port instead of a cocktail before what we had already surmised might be an exacting luncheon. For Rosemary, apparently, had encountered this Continental custom before.

I must pay my tribute at once to the way that meal was cooked and served. With the hors-d'œuvres, about twenty varieties, the manservant poured us out a white Corton 1923. As he did so, he formally announced, over each glass, the name of the wine, and the date. I could not help remarking how pleasant this was, to be officially allowed full consciousness of what one was eating and drinking, instead of keeping up at all costs a hypocritical pretence that one thing on the plate and in the glass was as good as another. Our hostess's enormous brown eyes flashed approval. She said quite frankly that she could not think of a more interesting subject for conversation. . . . I must add, in case from this you get too solid a vision of her, that she looked like Mélisande in the wood, almost too slender for belief, and her creamy white skin suggested that she never was tempted by any other diet than lentils, lettuces, and cold spring water.

The hors-d'œuvres were followed by a most delicious ragout of sweetbreads and mushrooms. Beans were served as an in-between course, preceding a very tender chicken in a wonderful dark-brown *risotto*, soaked in livers, gravy, and raisins. Next, we had a sort of winy trifle, and then fruit. The amusing pattern of the dessert-plates had been designed, so they told us, by the artist — I forget his name — who used to do all the magic-lantern slides, familiar to the pre-cinema generation — my own — who were shown magic-lantern slides as a treat at juvenile parties.

I must confess that we were curious to know with what special vintage M. Jaboulet-Vercherre intended to impress us. It proved to be a Pommard 1906, following a Pommard 1911. I shall never again think slightingly of Pommard, as I confess I had done hitherto; the 1906, especially, was a most delicate and fine-flavoured Burgundy.

When we returned to the drawing-room for our coffee, our host went to a side-table where stood three bottles. "Will you have," he asked me, " Cordial Médoc, Benedictine, or a *fine* Champagne? "

" A *fine*," I replied promptly, and so did Rosemary.

M. Jaboulet-Vercherre beamed. "You have made the right answer! "

I had not known that we were being put to a test similar to that of Portia's suitors, but it was certainly a relief that we had, so to speak, selected the leaden casket.

The Cognac was 1848, and, needless to say, as superlatively good as everything else we had drunk in that household.

Afterwards they showed us over the de la Commaraine cellars, which had been the old château chapel. Certainly the French used up their religious ruins; the garage at Bordeaux where Humphrey had parked his car was once a church; and at Château Ausone I have already mentioned that we found a little graveyard converted into a vineyard.

M. Jaboulet-Vercherre carried a little silver tasting-cup, of a shape which he said was in use everywhere in Burgundy. He tapped some Château de la Commaraine Pommard of 1924 and 1925 for us to taste, but said that the best year for laying down was 1923. The cellars here were lit in a more modern and convenient fashion than any we had yet been shown, by an overhead electric-light bulb that slid along wires, so that you could move it with you as you walked.

As we approached the room of the great vats, an odour drifted towards us that seemed to me both familiar and incongruous — the smell of hot jam-roll! My perplexity was soon enlightened. Apparently a small hod of juice from every vat gets cooked; we saw a red-hot furnace and dancing flames in a shed in one corner of the courtyard. It was the boiling hot grape-juice which had that rich warm simmering smell of jam. M. Jaboulet-Vercherre explained the whys and wherefores of this process to me very carefully, but I was not quite able to get the hang of it.

All the vats were already full of juice, as the

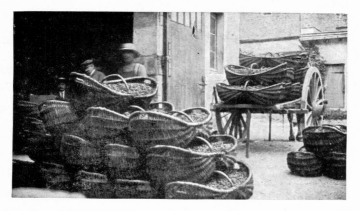

WEIGHING THE GRAPES IN BURGUNDY

THE CHAPEL IN THE VINEYARD—CHÂTEAU AUSONE

vintage was here in full swing; and everywhere — on the roads, up every alley, in the courtyards, and plunged wheel-deep among vines, were carts and brimming baskets of grapes, and busy men hoisting barrels up and down into the painted wine-carts.

Standing on top of the ladder to peep down for a glimpse over the rim of one of the vats, I was nearly overpowered by the rising fumes; and Madame, anxiously pleading for me to come down, told me how she had once found her husband lying insensible after a similar experience. Connoisseurs who simply drink the wine have no idea of the perils that lurk in wait for the wine-grower!

Madame told us furthermore, in reply to some of Johnny's questions, that, after four or five days' fermenting, the men would leap, naked, breast-high into the vats, to stir the grapes with their feet. Regarding this ceremony from, I swear it, a purely picturesque angle, I asked Madame if one might not be privileged to behold it. But alas, I shocked her! " It would not do for ladies to see," she said; " the men would *gênent* themselves! " . . . Ah well, we are a long time away from the pagan rites; from the exultant era when the votaries of Bacchus poured, leap-

ing and prancing, from the hills down into the valleys
to hail the vine-crowned god.

> And as I sat, over the light blue hills
> There came a noise of revellers: the rills
> Into the wide stream came of purple hue —
> 'Twas Bacchus and his crew!
> The earnest trumpet spake, and silver thrills
> From kissing cymbals made a merry din —
> 'Twas Bacchus and his kin!
> Like to a moving vintage down they came,
> Crown'd with green leaves, and faces all on flame,
> All madly dancing through the pleasant valley,
> To scare thee, Melancholy!

Certainly, in machinery and organization, the
cellars of M. Jaboulet-Vercherre were far from being
an orgy and a riot of primitive impulses. They were,
in fact, of the most up-to-date. But, after Keats, I
could not help remembering also, with a touch of wistfulness, Denys d'Auxerrois. . . .

The Jaboulet-Vercherres, untiring in their
bounteous entertainment of strangers, insisted that we
should return to the château for tea, before we drove
back to Beaune. The other three scored heavily on this;
for I, the elder lady-visitor, being served the first, was
asked whether I would take milk with my tea, or — I
could not quite make out what was the alternative of-

fered, except that it was in a bottle; and I feared that it might be some sort of *sirop*. But Humphrey and Johnny knew! they knew! — and Rosemary knew too, blast her! It was a biting cold day . . . and they had *rum* with their tea!

Then, with a great deal of ceremony and gaiety, and many elaborate speeches of thanks and farewell, we took our final leave of Monsieur and Madame. She, with a scarf thrown lightly over her shoulders, and her infant daughter in her arms, came down to see us off. The car stood in the drive, at the edge of the fountain, for Humphrey had contrived to draw it up on our arrival so that there was practically no option for me save to alight as a naiad, knee-deep into the shuddering pool.

Figure to yourself, then, the group in some detail; the gates of the Château de la Commaraine, the fountain, the departing English, the cordial French gracefully gesticulating good-bye. . . . I say the departing English, because the whole point of this description is that the English did *not* depart. . . . Not, at any rate, for about an hour. For the second time on our tour Flotsam had let us down, and that at a moment when we most wished to appear dignified, elegant, and debonair. I doubt if any book of deportment could have helped us through those horrible moments, while Madame smiled and chatted and assured us she was not catching cold — no, nor Bébé either; and we besought her not to remain outside to speed us. For, indeed, the temperature, under low-hung grey skies, could not have been far above zero.

M. Jaboulet-Vercherre, meanwhile, and his chauffeur, were peering into the innards of the car, trying to discover what was wrong, while Humphrey gloomily wished they wouldn't. The situation became ever more humiliating for us; and light and graceful conversation lapsed more and more into assurances from Rosemary that Flotsam never did this as a rule, and reassurances from Madame that she was quite sure of it. Jugs of very hot water were procured from the house, and poured into the radiator to warm Flotsam's engine. Flotsam stolidly took not the slightest notice. Rosemary and I were getting apprehensive about Humphrey's temper, which till then had stood the strain, but only just. At any moment we feared there might be a thin sharp snap, as of elastic strained beyond breaking-point, and then the Jaboulet-Vercherres would learn what this so charming, handsome, but rather reserved Englishman was really like.

The next suggestion was that the men of the party should push Flotsam from behind, and in this way get her engine hot enough to start. Thus, ignominiously and by hand — Rosemary and I ordered to remain in the car — were we shoved down the drive, out at the gates, and into the road. It was not quite the way in which we had hoped to leave the Château de la Commaraine; but after about ten minutes' shoving from behind, Flotsam actually did begin to move of her own accord, and we were able to drive away.

Our final backward view was of M. Jaboulet-Vercherre looking rather hot, and of his wife looking very cold. . . .

I do hope they still like us!

XXII
ROMANÉE–CONTI

IF you care at all about the sound of names, you
will want to drive at ninety kilometres an hour
down the hard sweep of the road through the Côte
d'Or, from Beaune to Dijon, on a thunderous purplish
afternoon, as we did; while Clos du Roi, Corton,
Charlemagne, Nuit Saint-George, Romanée La Tache,
Romanée-Conti, Richebourg, Clos Vougeot, Chambolle
Musigny, were announced arrogantly, as though blown
through trumpets, from either bank. For there is more
grandeur and resonance in the names of the great Burgundy vintages than in any others; and Romanée-
Conti, whither we were bound, is the noblest of them
all.

At the entrance of the narrow path which
branches off the great road to the left, to Romanée-
Conti, a group of gipsies had stationed themselves,

just beyond the notice saying that no gipsies were allowed in the Romanée precincts. It was queer that they should be there, and that that notice should be there and nowhere else. Was it just a coincidence, this haunting reminder of the ancient power of the Romans? Roumanians and the Romany race — a nation and a language, a race and a vineyard. . . . Well, there the poor Romanies squatted round their fires. They might not stray on to the Romanée lands, where kings bought their wines.

Monsieur Clin, or, if you prefer it, Simon the Cellarer again, received us with dignity, and showed us into a diminutive cellar, divided into two parts. The larger part held four or five dozen barrels of Richebourg. On the smaller side was the Romanée-Conti, about ten barrels of the 1924 vintage, already sold, and about thirty of 1925.

No more than that. . . . The least of the cellars we had hitherto visited in France could have held the Romanée-Conti *cave* ten times over. We were as awed, confronted by that impressive, that magnificently disdainful smallness, as we had been by the dim immensity of Château Margaux. . . . That great vaulted hall of a thousand casks, with its colossal pillars, and its wine-barrels lying on the floor in parallel row upon row, remains in my memory for ever, side by side with the simple inconspicuous little cellar of Romanée-Conti. Château Margaux could afford to be colossal. Romanée-Conti, no less, could afford not to be.

We tasted the Richebourg 1925, and then the Romanée-Conti 1924 and 1925. The '25 was less matured than the '25 Richebourg, but a fuller and more valiant wine.

Then M. Clin sent a man to take us out to the vineyard. The path wound up the slope, with vines on either side. Richebourg and Romanée Saint Vivant and *vin ordinaire*, all in communal neighbourhood . . . till our guide pointed out a patch not more than about four and a half acres in area, above and to the right of a cross.

"That is it," he said. "They are still the old French vines; not grafted," and he gave me a bunch to taste; a lighter, more pinkish purple than nine bunches out of ten. *Rosée* grapes, they called them, and they were sweeter than the others. He said that these, one out of ten growing there, added the special flavour to the rest.

It seemed inconceivable that the mere width

of a path should divide this rare and precious vintage from all the surrounding slopes of good, but less excellent wine.

And I wondered, too, why a cross should stand sentinel among none but richly pagan associations.

The best years of Romanée-Conti are 1899, 1906, 1911, 1915, 1919, 1923, and, as far as prophecy can commit itself, 1926; but there will be only an infinitesimal quantity of the last.

Perhaps the constant propinquity of that rare small vineyard, and those few sought-after barrels of Romanée-Conti, had its effect on the staff who worked there; for they also struck me as being unusually regal, simple, and severe; I felt shy at Romanée-Conti. They were polite, and they were cordial, but ——

—— But, in the Republic of France, they kept the key of the King's cellar.

XXIII
WE FEAR THAT WE MAY
FARE BADLY

"THEY shouldn't charge like princes and think like slaves! " remarked Humphrey, with a quality of lordly crossness in his voice. That was when we discovered on Saturday night that we wished to leave the hotel at Beaune on Sunday morning, and they had courteously refused our cheque, saying that they could not break a rule. So, while Rosemary and Johnny and I put together all the English money we happened to have, and all the Italian money as well as the French, in an attempt to make up the sum, Humphrey just sat there encouraging himself to get more and more angry.

" Of course," he argued, glaring at us, " they could easily break a rule if they dared trust their judgment. The first essential of a hotel manager," Humphrey went on, banging the table and stamping his foot, " is to have a swift instinct for character. Do I *look* the sort of man," thundered Humphrey, exasperated by our craven acquiescence, " do I look the sort of man whose cheque can't be taken in an emergency? "

Truth to tell, at that moment he looked the sort of man who ought to have been put under restraint. And though it was true that we had met a great number of hotel-keepers who had wisely and graciously trusted us on sight, yet it was quite unfair to accuse the hotel at Beaune of charging like princes. Our bedrooms and bathrooms had been among the most comfortable we had inhabited; and their charges on the whole were moderate, though the special food we had ordered worked out expensively.

They accepted our motley collection of notes of all countries, and we drove away looking haughty. The final indignant snort of Humphrey's horn was, I trust, not lost on the proprietor!

. . . And now we were driving south, away from the bitter chill of northern France, south to Mâcon, where a comfortable lodging and good wine and cooking awaited us at the Hôtel de l'Europe et de l'Angleterre. Rosemary was confident about this, re-

membering it from the last time she had sojourned
there in the spring. " You wait till you taste their
Romanée-Conti," she said.

. . . South, and then south again to Avignon,
and south to the Mediterranean and Italy. Nevertheless, we put up all the windows of the car, and were
still stiff and shivering, with that bluish feeling in our
blood — not blue, but bluish! — when we came into
the town. The roads had been magnificent all the way.

The Hôtel de l'Europe et de l'Angleterre stood
on the quay, facing the Saône. Rosemary's first moment of horror occurred when she saw that in front of
the hotel, and for a long way on either side of it, the
road was up, and workmen were digging a deep
ditch.

" I hope that doesn't mean — " she began. . . .
We drove straight into the courtyard of the
garage. She breathed a sigh of relief. The same garage-
man, anyhow! " It's all right! " For she was terribly
conscious of having exalted this hostelry to us, above
all others.

Hastening towards us from the hotel was a
very tall blond man in white linen. He had a high
forehead, sunny blue eyes, and a heavy sweep of fair

moustache. Beside him trotted a little dark woman, with a pleasant welcoming face.

"These aren't the proprietors," said Rosemary, but apprehensively. " At least, they weren't last time. It — it can't have changed hands? "

But it had changed hands, and only a fortnight ago. Moreover, so the new proprietor told us frankly, and most regretfully, there was no hot water in either bedrooms or bathrooms, because he was having an entirely new and up-to-date hot-water system put in; and everything was, for the moment, out of gear.

I think we would have gone on and tried our luck somewhere else but for two things: following the moment of confidence on seeing the garage-man, all our luggage had already been unloaded from the car; and Humphrey and Rosemary did not like to relinquish all hopes of that wonderful old Romanée-Conti, with which they were to quench our poor half-witted Bordelaisian notions of what good wine could be. But I could see that Rosemary was upset; and, indeed, none of us were feeling too happy at the notion of staying a night in this cold grey weather where there were no hot baths procurable.

We were shown up to our rooms. It was a very old inn, and the broad wooden staircase ran in a sort of gallery on the first floor round the four sides of the courtyard. Partially concealed by a screen in this gallery, a busy crone was working a sewing-machine. Rosemary remembered she had been there in the summer, working a sewing-machine. . . . At the right period of the inn's high prosperity she would have worn a wimple, and the sewing-machine would have been a distaff.

To Rosemary and Humphrey was allotted the same bedroom that they had had last time; but we were put into an enormous apartment on the same floor, called the " salon-bedroom," which was almost entirely a salon, and hardly a bedroom at all. It held " salon " furniture in scarlet and plush and gold; and there were acres of parquet floor; and scenes from Venice and Naples painted into medallions on the decorated walls; and — we counted them — as many as seventeen electric lights, fixed into the glittering candelabras and central chandelier! Mirrors and tables in profusion. . . . And somewhere, lost in the middle distance, two small and humble beds; and, skulking inside a cupboard, a wash-basin, with hot and cold laid on — hot not working!

It was all atmospheric and imperial to a high degree, rococo and baroque and ornate and Second Empire. . . . But also extremely large and extremely cold, and it was a long time before I found anywhere to hang up my coat.

Twenty minutes past twelve! We had risen early, and eaten very little breakfast. We were cold — I may have said this before! — cold and disappointed. By " we " I mean Humphrey, Johnny, and myself. Rosemary was all these things, only twice as much. You see, she had been the advance agent of the Hôtel de l'Europe et de l'Angleterre, as it had been under its former management. Now — who knows?

— " Well, for heaven's sake let's lunch, at any rate! "

We were hungry. . . . I may have mentioned this before.

We went downstairs. "*On peut déjeuner?*" confidently, to the *patron*, who stood in the hall.

"*Hélas, madame* — not for half an hour yet. Summer time ended last night, but perhaps *les messieurs* forgot to put back their watches? "

. . . Speechless, we walked on to a covered glass veranda outside the dining-room. The Saône shivered greyly outside. The *patron* added the unnecessary intelligence that the staff were still at their dinner. Apparently it was a very happy staff, and they were having a very good dinner. We could hear their bursts of laughter and merry voices from quite near by; drifts of succulent smell floated in to us. Bitterly, Rosemary hoped that they would not hurry on our account. Johnny wandered about vaguely, and tried to find a waiter who would bring us vermouth. Rosemary asked Humphrey to go up and fetch her fur coat.

— Well, of course we had been fools to forget summer time. It did strike us now, on looking back to it, that Beaune had not seemed properly awake and stirring when we drove through it, as we thought, at nine o'clock.

New management, no hot baths, and a long wait for lunch. . . . " I'm never going to recommend any place again! " said Rosemary, vehemently. She was not very far from angry tears. " Never again! This is what always happens if I do. I wish we hadn't stopped. I expect the cooking's frightful. I don't suppose there'll be any Romanée-Conti. This is what always happens! "

The half-hour passed. Midday chimed from the church towers of Mâcon. The staff, still laughing and cheerily talking, and obviously replete, began to stream upstairs from below, and to diffuse themselves through the deserted hall and dining-room, making them appear rather more normal. The waiter brought our vermouths.

We entered the dining-room. Rosemary immediately recognized, with a faint dawn of hope, the same head waiter, handsome, melancholy, Spanish-looking, who had served them so well in the summer.

And standing by our table was the *patron*, in his white linen jacket, bowing beside a vast *terrine de perdreau*.

(... " Things are looking up! " said the cat's-meat man.)

But Rosemary was not so easily lulled and appeased.

" Have you kept the same chef who was here when we came last year? " she asked.

Mine host shook his head. " He was not so good, that cook! "

Rosemary flushed angrily. Disappointment, cold, and hunger had upset her usually gracious manner. " He was *joliment* good enough," she said. " I can tell you, he was good enough for us! "

A queer little smile twisted the man's blond moustache. " My present cook, he is better."

Rosemary shrugged her shoulders. It was obvious that she would need a good deal of convincing. If this person had not come along a fortnight ago, upsetting the baths, sacking the cook, reorganizing the summer time . . . so her gesture implied.

M. Burtin moved away.

We ordered our wines from the head waiter; a Moulin à Vent 1919, which was more or less a wine of the district, and a Musigny of 1915. We decided that the Romanée-Conti should be left until dinner; for it *was* still on the wine-list, though to Rosemary's astonishment it proved to be no older than 1919; the melancholy waiter, who remembered her, assured her on his honour that it was the same date and vintage that she had drunk before.

We fell upon our *terrine* like wolves. It was a marvellously good *terrine* . . . but I had known that it would be, from that instant when I had seen mine host standing beside it with his knife and fork. There had been a curious suggestion of efficiency, of confidence, about his poise. The large dining-room was crowded, and he was busy. He did not come near us until we had finished the soup, and were half-way through the fish.

By this time, of course, we knew. . . .

"*Eh bien?*" There he was again, smiling at us in benign fashion.

"You were right," Rosemary confessed, frankly and generously. "That other cook was good, but this one, the one you have now, he is an artist, a *cordon bleu!*"

"It is my son," said M. Burtin. "I taught him."

. . . Suddenly his glance singled me out, I cannot tell why. He lowered his voice: "Can you understand German?"

"Yes."

He spoke German. "I was the cook of the Emperor Wilhelm."

XXIV
—BUT WE FARE IMPERIALLY!

I WONDER if to most people the magic and romance contained in the word " Emperor " is destroyed by the word " Wilhelm " following it? Not
yet, I suppose, can it be hoped that the War has
slipped among old wars, faded banners, forgotten
scars. And yet, just then, at that dramatic avowal,
Germany seemed no more malignant than Ruritania.
I have owned frankly that I love rant, and here was
unmistakably a grand first growth of rant. For this
man was entirely simple and straightforward; he took
it for granted that we and others would appreciate him
as a marvellous chef, and not deprecate his art because
England and Germany, or, if you will, because France
and Germany, had once been at war. Besides, there
was no more Emperor; only a white-haired old man
somewhere in Holland, with the disparaging syllable
" ex- " before his title.

After his first announcement M. Burtin did not mention the Emperor again; though he said, with a touch of honest wistfulness, that " those " had been a happy ten years in his life . . . and we talked a little of Vienna, Salzburg, Ischl, whither, no doubt, he had travelled with the staff whenever the Emperor of Germany had met King Edward of England, on their way to visit the Emperor of Austria, before Tweedledum and Tweedledee had agreed to have a battle. No doubt he had been recalled in 1914 to fight on the French side, for he was a Burgundian by birth. That was why, after an in-between sojourn at Seaulieu, he was now at last realizing what no doubt had been his persistent ambition from childhood upwards, to own an hotel not far from where he had been born, and to make it the best hotel in France — perhaps the best hotel in Europe, of its kind. He wanted it, he said, to be above all things *gemüthlich*; a comfortable, cheery, hearty inn, with a reputation for a good welcome and good food at all times and hours — " And plenty of laughter," he added, with hearty sentimentality — for those of every nation motoring along the great main roads to pass through Mâcon from north to south, and from east to west. He believed entirely in the good

old tradition of family unity in the business. Both his
sons were in the kitchen; he was obviously very proud
of them. His daughter-in-law, too, and his wife, were
putting all their energy and love into helping him to
run the hotel. It was quite plain to see that he got on
well with the Spanish-looking waiter whom he had
kept on; and, from a later moment of conversation
with his wife and the wall-eyed chambermaid, I
gathered that the latter had been with the couple for
six years, had followed them from Seaulieu, and fully
intended to stop with them all her life.

You could feel that the right spirit was abroad
in all the rooms above and below; and, indeed, the
peerless cooking and willing service must already
have won renown. Rosemary said the dining-room had
not been one quarter as full last time she had passed
through; outside clients, practically all of them. The
proprietor helped to wait on them; and contrived, we
could see, that each party should enjoy that feeling of
personal intimacy with him which is so valuable in
flattering our self-conceit. Who would not more gladly
be recognized, after a lapse of years, by a commis-
sionaire or a *maître d'hôtel* than by the Lord Chan-
cellor on the woolsack?

To come back to our dinner, which we watched now with the impersonal curiosity accorded to some significant pageant, as well as with the personal zest of appetite:

Following the *terrine de perdreau,* and a truly marvellous pike in creamy sauce, came partridge, served curiously with cabbage, slices of sausage, small rolled sausages, and potato balls. It was a good instinct which gave us this excellent but bourgeois cooking on top of the gourmet's fish. Next we had cheese. Then *tarte de la maison,* which I at once recognized as a typical and most delicious Viennese *Aprikosentorte* — slices of fruit on a huge open round of flaky pastry. With the fruit, appeared a different sort of *Torte,* again recognizable in origin; chocolate and nut, the very perfection of richness; and a dish of little crisp, curly biscuits. The coffee was all that coffee should be. As for the wine, the Moulin à Vent was perfectly sound and likable, but I have drunk better. Then followed the tragicomedy of the Musigny, which coincided so unfortunately with the entrance of the Dodos. . . .

The Dodos, male and female, had waddled across the room and established themselves at the table directly behind ours, before we realized the awfulness of what had happened. I cannot remember why we at once christened them the Dodos, except that they struck us as birds that ought to have been extinct. In their way they were ravishingly typical, fat and profiteerish. They both wore motor helmets and goggles, and she, in addition, had on several magenta coats, one over the other. They brought in a whiff from that quaint period when very few people possessed automobiles, and those that did changed into very special and elaborate costumes to sit in them. They drove a Sports Peugeot, striped red and black. They were accompanied by a horrible little yapping griffon. And they ordered, with much *empressement*, and drank with noisy pleasure, a wine that was pink and sparkling, and, I think, was alluringly labelled " Rosy Dawn."

The main distress about them was that the female Dodo, by her lavish use of powder and perfume, in her toilet *at* the table, before lunch, tossed great streams of odour upon the air, which rushed under Rosemary's nose just as she was about to take her first sip of Musigny. She swore that she could taste nothing, smell nothing, appreciate nothing but Dodo in her

Burgundy. We all suffered from it, but none so badly
as Rosemary, who was nearest to their table. The Dodos were, in their way, an æsthetic pleasure to us, but
I wish they had chosen a less famous and expensive
wine to extinguish. Had we, too, been drinking Rosy
Dawn, it would not have mattered.

However, one Dodo, or even two Dodos, do not
spoil a banquet. Our luncheon was glorious and unforgettable, and, in the light of M. Burtin's revelation, we
imagined that dinner would be of the quality and
quantity that ought to be encouraged by a walk beforehand. So, feeling rather Dodoish ourselves, but
determined to pay M. Burtin *fils* the compliment of
conquering our natural indolence, we waddled out to
explore Mâcon.

Mâcon proved to be an interesting little town,
with a ruined old thirteenth-century cathedral, one of
its towers ragged and upright, and the other broken
almost to the ground, with a cold gaping doorway between. We also discovered in one of the main streets
a sixteenth-century wooden house, tall and narrow,
with heavy doors and windows, and a fantastic pattern
of baboons carved across its façade. We glanced into
the more modern cathedral, seeing, for one vivid

moment, the impressive and well-staged tableau of benediction being celebrated at the altar. I cannot remember anything else about Mâcon, except that *The Rosary* was advertised as the great attraction at the theatre.

Towards five o'clock we still did not feel that we had shed enough of our earthly outlook to be able to look forward to renewing it at dinner; so while Humphrey strolled back to the inn, Rosemary and Johnny and I went for a walk — I am afraid, our first walk for four weeks! — over the bridge and along the towing-path beside the River Saône. It was very like an English autumn evening. The end of summertime had brought twilight dropping down long before we expected it. The air was warmer. Through the blue-grey haze, we watched the lights from the opposite bank swaying and breaking down the ripples of the water. Now and then we heard the plash of oars, a shout, an owl hooting in the poplars. . . . At about this time of day, and with just such sights and sounds, I had so often walked along the towing-path beside the Thames. Presently we turned and tramped more briskly back towards the bright bunch of lights that was Mâcon.

Somebody was talking to Johnny, asking him some vital question; a handsome gipsy child, who had run out from the caravans hidden among the trees — "*A quelle heure on commence, là-bas?*" She flung out a hand towards the town. I thought she meant vespers, but my mood was too melancholy and picturesque. She was inquiring at what time the cinema began!

M. Burtin greeted us in the hall. What a manner the man had — not manners, but a manner! He had caused a fire to be lit in the huge open fireplace of our salon bedroom; and Humphrey had tended it until it roared up the chimney, and flooded the vast spaces of the room with such friendly illumination that we had very little need of the seventeen lights in the candelabra and the chandelier.

Dinner, of course, was a flawless success. Things were in that vein, indeed, where nothing could fail. It was simpler than our lunch, which our host, in Continental fashion, apparently treated as the most voluminous meal of the day. We drank vermicelli clear soup, with some grated cheese that was not Parmesan; then sole, with an inspired velvety sauce, containing mushrooms and shrimps; next chicken, with *petits pois,* tomatoes, and potatoes; and then cheese.

I had sat down longing for a cocktail, for it is no good pretending that one never longs for a cocktail on a wine-tour, though of course such a desire must not be gratified, but stifled in its cradle. But I did need to begin with some drink that was sharp and ice-cold and refreshing; Chablis 1911 had all these elements, and was just exactly what I needed, though I believe by the judgment of the three others that it was not quite such a good Chablis as the perfect 1919 we had drunk at Beaune.

Next, and after a breathless pause, the Romanée-Conti 1919. . . .

I am a little bit hampered in my description of this Romanée-Conti by the knowledge that Humphrey and Rosemary, rampant Burgundians both, are waiting tensely, with the rod of criticism upraised in their hands, for what I shall say about it. For this to them was the wine of wines, and they were not disappointed in their second tasting of it, and in their display of it to us, as we had been disappointed over the Château Margaux 1899. It really was, Rosemary cried, exultant, and intoxicated by the mere fragrant breath of it, as good as ever. I remembered the superb disdain of that very little cellar I had seen, that — enormously little cellar. And, indeed, it was all that the finest and most superlative Burgundy could ever be, round, generous, velvety, full-bodied. . . . I am talking again in terms of sheer wine catalogue, but that can't be helped!

But — and I say this not defiantly, not from lack of appreciation, not to be cantankerous and ob- stinate, but from the very soul of my wine credo — I, the individual I, hereby proclaim once more, three heralds marching before me to clear the way, that I still find my felicity in the best Bordeaux, rather than in the best Burgundy.

And ever shall.

XXV
BACK TO THE RHONE

OUR sense of luck resilient held all the next day. The Burtin family and their devoted staff had made us feel, on regretfully saying good-bye to them, that here was a hostelry where we should always be remembered and welcomed whenever we came — ah, you must forgive the sob-stuff, but it fitted in with the tradition of Ruritania and the court of an ex-monarch, of Romanée-Conti, and of the huge formal salon with its plethora of winking lights. Whenever we came, M. Burtin assured us anew, both his hands warmly gripping mine, and his handsome blond person towering above me with blue-eyed benevolence, there should be our room waiting for us, and our table, a bottle of the best wine, and great gladness in all their hearts.

Incidentally, our bill was not staggeringly cheap. We had not really expected that it would be.

Burtin was not still cooking for kings, but nor did he intend to cook for paupers. He was a solid man, with solid ideas; and there was little doubt but that, when reconstruction had taken place, and he had his star in Michelin and the reputation he deserved, travellers by car would come twenty or thirty kilometres out of their way for a meal at his hotel. Foreigners have this laudable respect for comfort and superlative food; and so has the Englishman abroad, though not in England. In England he would not dream of swerving half a mile from his direct route, not even to lunch at the hotel of an emperor's *cordon bleu*. He would say, very sensibly: " My dear, it is not on our way! "

We assured M. and Mme Burtin that we had decided to make a pilgrimage to Mâcon every year, for the sake of sleeping one night and eating one meal at the Hôtel de l'Europe et de l'Angleterre — an odd name this, implying that England is apart from Europe and not included in it, which somehow one has often felt oneself! And Madame cried: " Ah, but you must not tell him that. He is so conceited already, and I can see him growing more and more conceited! " . . . And M. Burtin laughed and kissed her, and I think for two pins he would have kissed Rosemary and me, too, not to mention Humphrey and Johnny. It was plain to see that affection and cordiality were not merely and ostentatiously on the surface in this house, but that they were the actual power-station of all its comfortable efficiency.

" I should like to have seen that man in chain-armour," remarked Rosemary, as we drove away, waving our hands to the group at the door of the court-yard.

The road was hard, and the weather was bright, and we rushed at fine speed to Lyons, which astonished me by proving to be a beautiful old town, built pictur-esquely on either side of the impetuous Rhone. Some-how I had always featured Lyons in my mind as a sort of French Sheffield; factory chimneys, and busy thoroughfares, and rather obese silk-merchants; and a station where it was always dark and ghostly, as the Paris-Lyons-Méditerranée express slowed into it at night. . . . A few trucks clanked, and porters shouted — echoing hollow sounds. . . . You turned over in your *wagon-lit*, looked at the time, and fell asleep again. Paris-Lyons-Méditerranée . . .

But it was much more fun travelling by car. Finding the way into Lyons was a sweating business for Johnny, who held the map of the town and directed Humphrey. Humphrey wanted to go straight to a certain garage for some Fiat repairs; and, of course, in Lyons there were at least fifty garages. Also, Humphrey, on being directed wrongly through a strange town, where the turnings and the tram-lines and the prohibitions created a confused hell, was apt to lose his temper in a particularly biting, irritable style; following a condemnatory silence, he would say things like: " I may be half-witted, but granted even that, *and* driving the car, I had better take the map myself! " — And poor Rosemary, or poor Johnny, whichever of the two had been doing his best, would forthwith fumble out apologies, and attempt to retrieve his errors, and beg Humphrey to be nice and kind again, and forgive him, and consider his difficulties. . . .

So it will be believed that Johnny's breath came hard and quick, and his voice was clenched, as, reading the map of Lyons, he spoke his directions to the man at the wheel. There was one ghastly moment when Rosemary and I knew, by an indescribable something in his accents, that he had gone wrong; and we sat rigid with nerves, waiting for Humphrey's ex-

plosion. . . . But Johnny, by a series of brilliant con-
volutions, put him on the right road again, without
having to explain, or stop, or turn the car; and guided
him faithfully and truly up an almost invisible lane,
and straight into the Fiat garage.

We alighted. Humphrey gave Johnny a look
which very nearly resembled approval. " Good! " he
said, briefly. Then: " You're sweating! "

Johnny answered: " ' Nay,' the soldier's pride
touched to the quick, he said: ' I'm killed, Sire! ' And
his chief beside, smiling the boy fell dead."

— However, he revived when he saw the menu
at the two-star Restaurant Sorret, where we went for
lunch. There were three-star and four-star restaurants
at Lyons, but though we did not visit them, I find it
difficult to imagine anything better than the Sorret.
The *terrine de la maison,* with chicken truffles, *foie
gras,* and partridge contained therein, was in itself a
sufficient and a marvellous meal; and with it we drank
white Pouilly *en carafe,* which we called " the other
Pouilly," as distinct from Pouilly-sur-Loire. This was
the best wine I have ever had from carafe.

With our next course, *tournedos Rossini,* we
had returned to an old love, and chosen white Her-

mitage 1915. *Tournedos Rossinis* are those succulent, tender little steaks with a slice of *foie gras* on top of each, and a truffle nestling in the *foie gras*. The first time I ever had them — I must occasionally allow myself the Heavily Reminiscent style! — was at supper at the Bristol, in Vienna, after we had been to the Viennese Opera House to hear *Rosenkavalier*. . . . What a night of all-round perfection that was!

Our appetites were not in their usual form at the Sorret, which was a great pity, considering the number of times in the future when doubtless we should long for the *tournedos Rossini* that we then could not even finish!

After the Cognac and coffee, Johnny and I leaned over the balustrade of the bridge at Lyons, and watched alternately the water that flowed underneath, and the people who crossed to and fro, while we waited for Rosemary and Humphrey to return from some mysterious shopping. This revealed itself, when they presently rejoined us, as a gorgeous kimono of Lyons silk, flame-coloured and Chinese blue, which was formally presented to me, there on the bridge, as a token of regard, in memory of the wine-tour.

There was a sadness in this official recognition that the wine-tour was near its end; to banish it I shook out the blue and flame like a banner on the breeze; and the sun shone brightly down upon it, and the Rhone murmured: " Gaudy, but not neat," as it tore under the bridge down to Avignon and the sea. And the hurrying passers-by stared, and murmured: " *Les Anglais!* "

Were we to make a list in order of merit of all the roads on which Flotsam had run her course between Avignon and Avignon, our road that day from Lyons as far as Vienne would proudly take first place. Straight and true we flew along, hardly needing to slacken from our fifty-five miles an hour. Two or three times we touched sixty. The air was softer and warmer now. We were perceptibly going south, and recognizing familiar ground; here were the rustling patches of Indian corn, and all the lusher vegetation of the Midi and Provence. But we did not see the silvery tremble of olives again until we were beyond Montélimar.

Perhaps it was just as well that we were nearly home. I was more than half-way through *The Last Chronicle of Barset*, and I had arranged with myself that Trollope's six volumes of the Barchester series should just roundly last me the tour, no less and no more. If ever I do a tour in England — say, an ale-tour! — I shall read nothing but Balzac or Marcel Proust!

XXVI
THE LAST DRINK TOGETHER

VIENNE I remember mainly for the first sight of the evening light pouring in a warm saffron glow across its early Gothic cathedral, which stood high above the Rhone. On our other side, floating on the water, and moored up against the bank, was the material as opposed to the spiritual: a clumsy, friendly-looking washing-barge, with the busy women kneeling at the rim of it, washing the clothes in the river and spreading them to catch the last rays on the cabin roof. These floating laundries are fairly common on the Rhone. We had seen several. Like the Roman wine-carts, each one has its inevitable dog, sleeping on the cabin-roof, among the odd-shaped patches of white and blue and pink and bright scarlet.

There was still time that evening, after we had unloaded, to drive to Ampuis, to see the slopes of

Côte Rôtie. We had been told to ask for the barrel-maker, Colombet; but his house stood a little way outside the village, and at first we had some difficulty in finding our way to it. We were instructed over and over again that M. Colombet lived " over the bridge, and then ask and inform yourselves again, and then, when you turn, it is the last house. . . ." So that we were astray in a bewilderment of narrow lanes. A man came towards us on a bicycle, quickly pedalling in the opposite direction. We called out to him, asking the way to M. Colombet's house. He stopped, and sprang off his machine at once, looked at our card of introduction, and, explaining that he was a stranger in that part of the country, took our card and said that he would ride with it back again to the village, and get clear directions for us, thus relieving us of the necessity of turning the car. His manner was merely courteous, not in the least officious. He came back again in a few minutes, and told us exactly where to find the house we wanted. No doubt his *croix de guerre,* and the *médaille militaire,* which latter can be won only by private soldiers and generals commanding armies, had been gained for rather more dashing exploits than this; nevertheless, there was no need for

him to take all this trouble for strangers and foreigners and we appreciated it. It was typical of the
treatment we had met throughout France.

Colombet was a charming old man. You could
not forbear from loving him at first sight of his kind,
peering eyes, and slow, rather puzzled, smile. Without
stopping to take off his apron, for he was working in
his own little vineyard when we drove up to the house,
he took us along the road till we could see the whole
of the hill of Côte Rôtie. It was so steep that little
steps were cut in the walls from terrace to terrace, and
these terraces were frequently too narrow for more
than one row of vines.

Colombet, after protesting shyly for some
time, allowed himself to be persuaded, when we got
back to Ampuis, to sit down outside a café and share
a bottle of Côte Rôtie with us. Little by little he became, so to speak, acclimatized to our presence, and
talked with a sincere and lovable patriotism, placing
the delicacy of his own Côte Rôtie wines far above the
more " *grossier* " Hermitage. But he said that the
Côte Rôtie growths had lost more finesse by grafting
than any other wine in France. He could remember
the pre-phylloxera period, though he was but a child

then. . . . And he remembered it, gently, for some time, sitting there in the soft twilight, while we attentively listened. . . .

His reminiscences merged, I know not how, into a heroic figure he was building up for us, anecdote by anecdote; this Monsieur So-and-So, thus ran the legend, who was the grandfather of some local personage, had a swifter intuition for second growths than any who had lived before or since in the Côte du Rhône regions: "He never touched first growths," said Colombet, his admiration expressed in strong dialect, so that we found it hard to understand him; "never! He left them alone. But, *mon Dieu*, what a palate for the second growths! Not once did he make a mistake. Nowadays these owners, they know a little about wine, yes, and they learn a little more — perhaps. But he — he *knew!* "

As for Côte Rôtie itself, I was not very fond of it; but I believe, nevertheless, it is a good wine if you happen to have a fancy for its characteristic flavour.

At dinner that night, at the Hôtel du Nord, we sampled a Saint-Joseph, also a very good red Rhone wine, with a pronounced bouquet, which I preferred to the Côte Rôtie. We had as a vegetable course quite a pleasing, though homely, dish of sliced *aubergines* and tomatoes, stewed together; but otherwise the hotel was indifferent.

On the next day, October 5th, the luggage was strapped on the back of Flotsam for the last time during that tour, for we expected to arrive at Avignon in the evening. From Avignon Humphrey and Rosemary were going on by car, after one night's rest, to Antibes, where Johnny and I would rejoin them by train a couple of days later; for we had to wait at Avignon for the arrival of the Siamese cats from Beaune.

On the long day's run through the dear hill-bound valley of the Rhone, I found myself collecting, within the four walls of memory, those glimpses of faces upturned for a second as we rushed past. . . . There had been hundreds during the last five weeks, but perhaps half a dozen had made some curious personal appeal to me, so that I could still see them clearly, while the rest were forgotten even as we whirled away out of their ken. But here and there a gesture just caught, a curve of the head, a swift look from a pair of eyes that one would never be likely to encounter again . . .

Two children, for instance, I think it was at Arles, sitting beside each other on the door-step of an old house in a sombre alley nibbled by the sunshine. They were exactly alike: round brown heads, round brown eyes, faded red frocks, round red mouths that breathed: " Oh! " as we tore past. . . . How pretty they were — and how round!

And then that other child, cheering from the back of a snow-white donkey, charging us, he must have thought, down the very centre of a broad road, on one of those bright days of autumn. And he looked at us, too, and defied us valiantly, laughing at danger. His hair was very gold, and the donkey, as I said, was very white, and he was undoubtedly acting from the very centre of some martial dream. . . .

And then there was that wild-looking, lost-looking, shepherd-boy, a character stepped straight out of the pages of Walter de la Mare; and I received from his eyes some strange forlorn appeal, mixed with anger. And after, when I had remembered and forgotten him, I remembered the old man with the leathery skin, sitting, Chinese and inscrutable, in the doorway of his shop, where nothing was sold but wooden clogs. . . . The clogs were piled up high around

him, into a frame, and we were trying to turn Flotsam, in the little *place* just outside; and he sat motionless and watched our agitated gyrations and backings
and gear-changings. I felt that he was amused. We
were so active and feverish, and he and his clogs so
passive and acquiescent. . . .

Were there no more faces that brimmed up,
significantly, out of the crowd of faces, mostly astonished, mostly a little resentful, as quiet pedestrians
are still wont to be when a motor-car rushes by them,
hooting? Yes, a fierce little village girl of perhaps
twelve or thirteen years, with that thin promise in
her looks of great beauty one day, of vivid, consum-
ing, intellectual beauty. Of course they called her
plain, now. You could see that she suffered because
of her plainness, and her thinness. I should like to
have talked with that little girl. Her big seeking eyes
sped a message to everyone on the road who tore past
her, free to go where they pleased. . . .

And then I recalled a bridge, a small crooked
bridge — I wonder where that was? — and, just about
to open the gate and cross it, an old woman, with wide
white flaps to her cap, and the face of a jovial monk;
a bounteous, broad-minded lewd old monk. That white

cap, surely it was a disguise? I have never seen a woman's face so seamed with merry experience. And then her face, too, waltzed into limbo, with the shepherd-boy's, the clog philosopher's, the children. . . . There is nothing to tell why just those few should have marked themselves so clearly on my subconscious mind. We had whizzed by many a great bulging load of hay, on carts drawn by oxen; but there is only one I clearly remember; and that one, if I were an artist, I could draw for you, down to the most minute detail; yet it was like all the other swaying carts, loaded high with hay. . . .

The surface of the roads had been awful all that day, with hardly any decent patches to give us temporary relief from the jar and bump down into one pot-hole, and out again, and down into the next, and out and on and down again, so that the length of the way to Avignon appeared interminable. We were dead tired, and it was dark already, by the time we skirted round the Roman arch at Orange; and from Orange to Avignon was a nightmare of ill-lighted villages, and black roads, looming carts, and the sudden dazzle of other motorists' head-lights. And then a jumble of tram-lines. The strain was telling on Humphrey very considerably, but he was a fine driver, and eventually we were landed safely at our hotel in Avignon.

We were too shaken and tired to notice what we ate and drank for dinner that evening; our return was not quite of that calm rejoicing quality we had anticipated, skimming along beautiful roads, and arriving at sunset at Avignon, with a wistful sigh of regret because the tour was ended. In fact, the apotheosis and grand peroration had to be postponed until lunch the next day. Humphrey and Rosemary were departing directly afterwards.

So we lunched at the Restaurant Lance, where we had *brandade* again, and *perdreau rôti*, and drank Hermitage. We drank Hermitage because Johnny and I did not feel quite noble enough to suggest Burgundy, and neither were Humphrey and Rosemary sufficiently generous to plead for Bordeaux! Hermitage was common ground. We had all four agreed about its high merits. It was right and fitting that the Bordelais and the Burgundians should sink their lances to rest, and that the last toast should be drunk in harmony. . . .

And as we ate and drank, we discussed, in a rare mood, free from truculence, the different wines we had drunk, and which were the most memorable. The white Hermitage of 1874, of course, and both the red and white Hermitages of 1906, and the Château-neuf du Pape, white and red, which they had given us at the Restaurant Bellevue. And the Château Grillet 1874; and of the Bordeaux, alas, only Château Ausone, and that was a Bordeaux Saint-Émilion, not a Médoc. And Vouvray, Château Moncontour. And Pouilly-sur-Loire 1906. And the Chablis du Clos 1919, which we had drunk at Beaune. And Romanée-Conti 1919. No others were included in this final summing-up, for these were the patricians among wines, the kings and queens and ladies of quality.

My last words to Humphrey, as Johnny and I stood on the steps of the hotel, feeling utterly abandoned, deserted, neglected, jilted, forlorn, and forsaken, and saw Flotsam loaded up with their luggage, and not with ours, were to bid him have my cocktail ready when I should arrive the day after to-morrow at Antibes. . . . And suddenly a little thrill shot through my being, a thrill flavoured with Angostura and iced gin, as my imagination prophetically tasted this first most wonderful, most delicious cocktail, after the five weeks' haughty abstinence which connoisseurship had exacted of us.

XXVII
UP THE BORDELAIS!

JOHNNY and I dined tête-à-tête that night, at Hiely's.

We turned to the Bordeaux on the wine-list, and ordered a Château Latour 1914.

With the exception of the Château Ausone, it proved to be the best claret we had tasted on the tour.

But they would never believe us. . . .

A NOTE ON THE TYPE IN
WHICH THIS BOOK IS SET

This book is composed on the Linotype in Bodoni, so-called after its designer, Giambattista Bodoni (1740–1813) a celebrated Italian scholar and printer. Bodoni planned his type especially for use on the more smoothly finished papers that came into vogue late in the eighteenth century and drew his letters with a mechanical regularity that is readily apparent on comparison with the less formal old style. Other characteristics that will be noted are the square serifs without fillet and the marked contrast between the light and heavy strokes.

SET UP, ELECTROTYPED, PRINTED AND
BOUND BY THE PLIMPTON PRESS,
NORWOOD, MASS. · ESPARTO PAPER
MANUFACTURED IN SCOTLAND
AND FURNISHED BY W. F.
ETHERINGTON & CO.,
NEW YORK

Route of the "Flotsam"